THE GAME
OF OUR LIVES

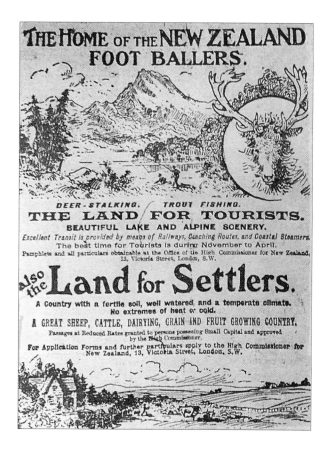

THE GAME OF OUR LIVES

The Television Series

Producer
George Andrews

Directors
John Carlaw
Alan Erson

Research
Finlay Macdonald
Tim Plant
Rachel Rushton

Film & Picture Research
Ann Andrews

Consultants
Robin McConnell
Ron Palenski
Warwick Roger

Editors
Bill Toepfer
Tim Woodhouse

Sound Designer
Chris Burt

Titles
Jules Clark

Production Design
Shayne Radford

Original Music
Stephen McCurdy

Principal Photography
Paul Richards

Additional Photography
Clinton Bruce
Swami Hansa

Location Sound
Leighton Clapham
Paul Chattington
John Patrick

Production Manager
Sarah Metcalfe

Narrator
Stuart Devenie

Network Executive
Tom Finlayson

THE GAME OF OUR LIVES

The story of Rugby and New Zealand —
and how they've shaped each other

Text: Finlay Macdonald

Photographs: Bruce Connew

Picture research: Ann Andrews

VIKING

VIKING
Penguin Books (NZ) Ltd, 182–190 Wairau Road, Auckland 10,
New Zealand
Penguin Books Ltd, 27 Wrights Lane, London W8 5TZ,
England
Penguin USA, 375 Hudson Street, New York, NY 10014,
United States
Penguin Books Australia Ltd, 487 Maroondah Highway, Ringwood,
Australia 3134
Penguin Books Canada Ltd, 10 Alcorn Avenue, Toronto, Ontario,
Canada M4V 3B2

Penguin Books Ltd, Registered offices: Harmondsworth, Middlesex,
England

First published by Penguin Books New Zealand, 1996

Editorial services by Michael Gifkins and Associates
Designed by Chris O'Brien, Pages Literary Pursuits
Printed in New Zealand

ISBN 0670 869074

Contents

Acknowledgements

This book, like the television series from which it is derived, would not have been possible without the generous help of many people. I am indebted to everyone interviewed for the four programmes in the series, some of whom did not make the final cut for reasons of time and space, but who do appear in this book. All are owed equal gratitude. In particular I would like to thank those whose own work in the fields of sporting and social history was invaluable in the preparation of the series and the book: Len Richardson, for his guiding wisdom and knowledge of the formative years of rugby in New Zealand; Neville McMillan, for his encyclopaedic knowledge of rugby history, and for his rugby encyclopaedias; Jock Phillips, for his insights into the implications of New Zealand's great passion for rugby; Ron Palenski, Warwick Roger and Robin McConnell for their interest in and association with the production of the programmes. I am also indebted to the many great chroniclers of rugby, some of whom are noted in the bibliography, without whom one would search long and hard for the dates, names and details that anchor so much speculation in the firmer ground of fact. Thanks are also due to my fellow researcher Tim Plant, and especially to Ann Andrews, without whose assiduous picture research the series and the book would have been immeasurably inferior. And finally I would like to acknowledge the help, generosity and good humour of Douglas Dalton, All Black forward of the 1930s, who died in his 83rd year during the filming of the series. They tell me he was a hard man in his day, but he was a gentleman to the end.

Finlay Macdonald

Introduction

'Rugby football was the best of all our pleasures,' wrote John Mulgan. 'It was religion and desire and fulfilment all in one.' At the time he was writing, during the Second World War, his words were undoubtedly true. But rugby had not always been so definitive an institution for New Zealanders, and it would not remain one forever. The story of how one game came to be embraced so passionately by a people, and how that embrace has slowly loosened, is also the story of a country's growing up. In much the same way that a child learns a game, becomes adept at it and then lives for it, and eventually grows up to find other things to do, New Zealand's progress from infant colony to adult society can be charted through its favourite game.

There can be few people in New Zealand whose lives have not been touched by rugby, one way or another. Good at the game or lousy, infatuated or bored rigid by it, male or female, rugby is too all-pervasive, too ubiquitous to have been avoided altogether. Love it or hate it, rugby is a metaphor. It can be used to define and describe the good and the bad of New Zealand society. Look hard enough at rugby's sometimes arcane rituals, and a picture does emerge of who we were, and why we are who we are; an answer of sorts to the question that ends Greg McGee's play *Foreskin's Lament*, 'Whaddarya?' Maybe it's a truism to say that a country's national game is a clue to its national soul, but there can be few better clues.

In rugby, New Zealanders have seen themselves. Like some strange muddied mirror, it has reflected what we wanted to see, and sometimes what we did not. Through peace and war, depression and social revolution, rugby has been a badge of identity. It has been a source of pride and shame. Far from home it can provide the warmth of recognition. It was something we were genuinely good at, not a cause to cringe. Whether you stood within its circle or defiantly without, rugby could never be ignored. Embraced or excluded by its cults and rites of passage, you could never remain indifferent. That is, until very recently. It is ironic, but perhaps not surprising, that rugby should begin rewarding its best

1

players with money at the point in its history when it can no longer lay claim to being a universal experience.

The television series upon which this book is based set out to look at New Zealand's social history through rugby. A very wise man once said that there is rightfully no history but biography, and so it is with rugby as a window onto the collective landscape. Like the series, the book is peppered with the anecdotes of several generations of rugby players, fans and even detractors. The reader need not agree with everything that is said. Indeed, one of the pleasures of grappling with the meaning of rugby is the absence of definitive conclusions. No one really knows exactly why this tiny corner of the British Empire fell in love so passionately with the oval ball, or why rugby came to represent an essential New Zealandness during its ascendant era. There are some facts, and there are theories, myths and legends. If the text betrays its origins as a series of television scripts, so be it. This is neither definitive social history, nor exhaustive rugby history. Both are done far better elsewhere. Rather, this is one story of how a game and its country shaped each other. And everyone will have their bit to add to the story of the game of our lives.

Part 1

ARRIVAL

The myth was that we were all but perfect practitioners of rugby. If we were beaten it was usually the fault of the referee. If we were beaten it was usually the fault of the selectors. If we were beaten it was usually the fault of some stupid bastard dropping a ball in the goal mouth. These were the currents of the myth which led to New Zealand and rugby being indivisible.

– *journalist T P McLean*

To speak of rugby in terms of myth is inevitable in a country for which the game has become a national symbol and an enduring obsession. Myths evolve to explain the present by describing the past, and so it is with rugby in New Zealand. From the moment of its arrival, the game wove itself into the fabric of an emerging settler society, and sent roots deep into soil pocked with the sprig marks of a million boots.

Myths are also fictions, of course. What might once have been observable fact becomes over time an elaborate construction of half-truth, memory, sentiment and embellishment. So too with rugby. At various times the tool of unscrupulous politicians, imperial flag-wavers and class-conscious élites, the game has been used as the symbol of a hearty colonial self-image, a badge of manly virtue and proof of racial harmony. In being asked to justify other myths, rugby itself became mythologised.

But where does the myth begin? How did a game for English gentlemen come to be the passion of an egalitarian society half a world away? How did a pastime of the leisured classes in Britain even manage to take hold in a land where few could afford to stop working? How did rugby become a mould in which national identity was formed? How did it become, in John Mulgan's words, 'religion and desire and fulfilment all in one'?

In trying to answer such questions, it is too easy to forget the most elemental truth about rugby. People play it because they like it. Whatever else has been invested in it, rugby is a communal pastime; the club a village well; the game a chance to meet, catch up, host and be hosted. In a land of few festivals, rugby has

Home and Away

been New Zealand's seasonal reason to celebrate. These are the other strands of the myth — the personal joys, the family traditions, the uncomplicated pleasures of banging into someone with a ball in your hands or standing on the sideline cheering them on.

For more than a hundred years rugby has provided many things, taking people to other places, small town to neighbouring small town, city to city, or finally to another country. Rugby has been the enemy of distance and separation. In the process, it has contributed to New Zealand's sense of national cohesion; provided, in the words of sociologist Geoff Fougere, 'unity out of diversity'. From the earliest days of rugby this was one of its crucial functions, taking local rivalries at the club level and assembling them into a common cause at the provincial level, and finally into mass allegiance to the national team (and icon), the All Blacks. Far from obliterating difference, rugby has used it to forge a larger whole.

. . . and of course we were all fans of the All Blacks.

> When I was growing up in Timaru the key teams were mapped onto lines of difference in the town. So one of the clubs was Marist — young men who had gone to Catholic schools. And it played a team called Zingari, which was very much a club for young Protestant men. Another line was between those who had got a high school education at the Boys High School to prepare them for white-collar work, and those who had got an education at the Technical School that largely prepared them for blue-collar work. They became the Old Boys Club and the Star Club.
>
> Then, of course, at the next level up, all of those differences were submerged. We were all fans of the South Canterbury team, and of course we were all fans of the All Blacks.
>
> *Geoff Fougere*

The origins of this social alchemy lie far from the untamed bush of nineteenth century New Zealand, on the playing fields of green and pleasant England. The intense bond with rugby is at least partly the result of historical coincidence. At the same time as the colony was being settled in earnest after 1840, the playing of organised team games in Great Britain was taking hold. This so-called games revolution found its way quite naturally to New Zealand, as the immigrant ships regularly departed and the wealthier members of the new society down-under began to send their sons and daughters home to be educated.

Victorian England was witnessing the great divergence of football codes, as soccer and rugby gradually differentiated and the rules (or laws) were agreed upon. Rugby gained a huge boost from the phenomenally popular novel *Tom Brown's Schooldays*, written in 1857 and on to its fiftieth edition within the lifetime

A game at Rugby School in 1852, five years before the publication of Tom Brown's Schooldays, *and eighteen years before the first recorded rugby game in New Zealand.*
NZ Rugby Museum

of its author, Thomas Hughes. Set at Rugby School in the days of its famous headmaster, Thomas Arnold, the book drew on current ideas about human perfectibility and aimed, in a very Christian way, to elevate as well as entertain the reader. Team games, the book suggested, were character-building and the ideal preparation for the defence of Empire (*Tom Brown* was published just after the Crimean War). The theme of 'muscular Christianity' was eagerly taken up by educators and politicians, who praised games as a way to impart the desirable attributes of manly virtue: acceptance of authority, perseverance against the odds, the ability to lead and to win or lose gracefully.

> It was a mask, really, for something else. On many occasions you had people whose real objective in the beginning of clubs or rugby teams was a form of naked social control. Headmasters in the various public schools of England, for example, were as much interested in keeping order in their schools as they were in creating manly gentlemen. But it didn't look good in discussing this matter with parents — that what you were trying to do was control these little gentlemen who were likely to run amok. Much better if you dressed up this sort of new team game phenomenon in some kind of ideological justification.
>
> *historian Len Richardson*

It was a mask, really, for something else.

The transfer of rugby from the old world to the new was not necessarily a haphazard affair. One of the founders of the New Zealand game, George Sale,

*. . . he picked up
the football and ran
with it . . .*

was actually born at Rugby School, where his father taught. Sale attended the school in the 1840s, and may have been on the committee that wrote the formal rules of rugby as played at the school in 1845 (some time after William Webb Ellis's apocryphal act of creation, whereby he picked up the football and ran with it, thereby giving the game its unique feature). Sale emigrated to New Zealand and became editor of the Christchurch *Press*, then a sheep farmer in Canterbury, a West Coast goldfields commissioner and finally foundation professor of classics at the University of Otago. And it was there, in 1870, that he helped kick off the game of rugby in the province.

He would undoubtedly have approved of the words of Pierre de Coubertin, founder of the modern Olympics, who wrote in his *L'Education anglaise*, 'When one is a squatter in New Zealand . . . one finds oneself well off to have received in the public schools such a strong physical and moral education. Muscles and morality are there the first object of necessity.'

Sale was a direct connection to the patrician, public school origins of the game. Yet New Zealand was anything but a replica of the society from which he came. By 1870 the land wars in Taranaki and the Waikato had barely ended, and Te Kooti was still waging a highly successful guerrilla war. The population of only 300,000 was growing rapidly as more British migrants arrived, and the

A New Zealand hunting party from the 1870s — another English tradition survives translation to the rough and ready colonial setting. It was men like these who turned rugby into the country's national game.
Kitching Collection, Nelson Provincial Museum

bush and scrub were being cleared fast for pasture. Wool would soon overtake gold as the colony's most valuable export, and the gold rush was shifting from the West Coast to Thames. Already, Australian gold miners had imported their own version of rugby, Victorian Rules, which was hugely popular by the time 'real' rugby arrived.

Victorian Rules borrowed heavily from rugby, but had emerged in the 1850s when the various forms of English football were still changing and developing. When the gold-fuelled boom in Victoria started to wane in the 1860s, thousands of young fortune hunters boarded small steamships for the South Island of New Zealand, taking their game with them. As Australian historian Geoffrey Blainey has observed, the South Island was 'in commerce almost a province of Melbourne', and the sport played reflected this. In Dunedin, then New Zealand's largest city, Victorian Rules and rugby lived uneasily side by side for some years, with the Dunedin Club (favoured by Scots immigrants) playing rugby, and the Union Club playing the Australian version. In 1876 the two clubs played a match in which the first half was played under rugby rules and the second under Victorian rules.

Victorian gold seekers believed their game might take over in New Zealand, but as migration increased from Britain, and economic power shifted to the north and Auckland, with its closer links to Sydney, rugby quickly squeezed out the rival code — no doubt much to the relief of rugby evangelists like George Sale.

> ... this colonial, bastardised version which was being imported ...

From their point of view the game they wanted to sink deep roots in New Zealand was the grand old game that they'd learned at home. But here was this colonial, bastardised version which was being imported across to Otago and Auckland, and everywhere, being played quite strongly throughout the country for rather longer than some New Zealanders like to admit, I suspect.
Len Richardson

THE FATHER OF NEW ZEALAND RUGBY

Despite Sale's undisputed role in establishing rugby in its new home, the title of father of New Zealand rugby is usually given to Charles John Monro, son of the English-born New Zealand parliamentarian and speaker of the House, Sir David Monro. On his sixteenth birthday in 1867 young Monro, like many of his peers, was dispatched home to England to complete his education. He attended Christ's College in Finchley, North London — by all accounts a place of cold dormitories

Charles Monro (right), son of New Zealand's Speaker of the House of Representatives, and the acknowledged father of New Zealand rugby.
W E Brown Collection, Nelson Provincial Museum

. . . *we were the pioneers of New Zealand's national game.*

8

and bad food, but already one of the leading rugby-playing public schools in England. Monro was 18 when he returned aboard the trader *Airedale* with the laws of rugby in his suitcase.

In his native Nelson he found his old friends still playing soccer or Victorian football, but within months had convinced the Nelson Football Club and his old school, Nelson College, to try the new game. The first recorded game of rugby in New Zealand took place on 14 May 1870, at Nelson's botanical gardens. Charles played and Sir David and Lady Monro were among the spectators. Later that year, Monro took his team to Wellington for the first away game. Having scouted a suitable playing field on the Petone foreshore, he selected the Wellington side himself, and through his father's connections arranged for the Nelson team's transport across Cook Strait on the government steamer *Luna*. (Rugby might yet become a symbol of egalitarianism, but friends in high places have always made a difference.) Wrote Monro of the game: 'There was no referee with his confounded whistle to check almost every heroic effort, but Lord did we enjoy ourselves! And how little did we think that we were the pioneers of New Zealand's great national game.'

Monro bought land near Palmerston North and established a sheep farm called Craiglockhart, after his grandfather's estate in Scotland. He married in 1885 and fathered three sons and two daughters. His grandson, Peter Gaisford, who now lives in Opotiki, remembers the old man well, having been raised in the large house at Craiglockhart from an early age. Monro, says Gaisford, was patriarchal but affectionate, with a predilection for growing fruit trees, and was a dead shot with a stone if he caught anyone poaching from his orchard. He was also mildly eccentric, having once imported Chinese fire-crackers to insert in the frames of hanging pictures as an early form of fire alarm; the theory being that the explosions would wake or alert the household to the danger before the house was consumed in flames.

As for Monro's status as 'father of New Zealand rugby', Gaisford says he never spoke much of it; the one exception being when Robert Tennent, a founder

*Members of the Wellington
Rugby Club in the 1870s, their
matching uniforms a sign of the
game's rapid organisation.*
Bill Brien

*Robert Tennent (with his wife),
contemporary of Charles Monro
and fellow pioneer of New
Zealand rugby.*
Isaacs and Clark Collection,
Nelson Provincial Museum

of the Nelson Football Club, made a similar claim and some vigorous correspondence was entered into. 'I think we were more proud of him for being the father of rugby than he was,' says Gaisford. 'And more glory was reflected on us than he ever claimed for himself.'

Modesty aside, Monro was a pioneer of rugby in a pioneer country. Like Sale, he also embodies the contradictory nature of rugby in New Zealand: a public school game embraced by a nation colonised by the downstairs classes; born on England's green fields, but ideally suited to a rough-and-ready land, easy to play on makeshift grounds; invented by and for the aristocracy, but a great mixer of men away from the hidebound class system of home.

Rugby was the common factor in the getting together, but it provided for social intercourse beyond purely rugby. The butcher and the doctor, for example, might talk after the game about something other than rugby or about

their own occupations. Without rugby as the catalyst, the opportunity would never otherwise have arisen.

journalist Ron Palenski

They cut down trees, they built up farms and they were very hardworking men, and rugby was the ideal game for men of those sterling muscular qualities. Jesus Christ, if you spend six and a half days a week slogging your guts out, you must have some relief, and rugby, with its slight traces of violence and so on, was wonderful. Blokes were knocking each other over for the pleasure of doing so, and having a beer afterwards in the friendliest possible way.

T P McLean

A GAME WORTHY OF SAVAGES?

There can be no doubt that rugby suited the lifestyles and the landscape of early settler New Zealand, and would have found fertile soil in a community where half the adult men were unmarried and in search of institutions to make their own. But here we encounter the myth again. Frontier societies have always tended to portray themselves in epic terms; in this case, of rough, tough men clearing the land, forging a new world out of the bush, playing a rough, tough game to match the honest toil of their working lives. In fact, a hard physical game was not the best pastime for men engaged in hard physical labour. The same myth has been used to explain the origins of Victorian football, which it is often assumed was born on the goldfields. But as Geoffrey Blainey has argued, 'It would be . . . surprising if young men who were excitedly digging for gold or travelling across country to the latest rush should begin to play regularly a game that required energy and time and that involved the risk of injuries that could prevent them from digging for gold.'

As in Australia, the first men who took to rugby in New Zealand were generally those who worked at desks in offices. Insurance clerks, bank staff and postal workers were at the forefront of the formation of the first rugby clubs. These were the men who needed and could afford physical release in a game, not those who were slogging in the backblocks with axe and pit-saw. Similarly, the early clubs are urban, which again gives the lie to any notion that rugby emerged miraculously from the bush. Town dwellers could easily organise a team or a game, whereas in isolated rural areas men lived for months on end without contact.

Robert Tennent, the Nelson contemporary of Monro who worked for the

Blokes were knocking each other over for the pleasure of doing so . . .

1.
The Saturday ritual. Young spectators watch Waiau Star play Balfour at Tuatapere, Southland, 1995, followed by the other ritual, when both senior teams sit down in the Waiau clubrooms to watch the All Blacks play Australia.

2.
*Running repairs with
an audience of one.
Rugby as family affair
at Tuatapere.*

3.

Rugby's real story begins here, away from the grandstands and the crowds. A father teaching his son to kick a ball. Like his son Matthew, Steven Edgerton learnt about rugby from his father. His club, Waiau Star of Tuatapere, is over 100 years old.

4.
Fathers and sons: the key to rugby's enduring appeal. Aaron and Robert Wilson (right) are the latest in a long family line to have played for the local club. Says Robert: 'We stick together. We live in a country area, we travel by bus, we travel home by bus together as a team . . . No, we're pretty much a team for the whole day when we play rugby.'

Otago University's first fifteen in the 1880s – likelier early stalwarts of the game than bushmen and gold diggers.
Hocken Library

Bank of New South Wales, is a perfect example of the early rugby pioneer. Moving around on various postings, he took the laws of rugby with him, pollinating the country as he went. The truth is, rugby moved outward from the towns into the countryside as New Zealand was gradually opened up by road and rail. Indeed, rugby's arrival coincided almost exactly with the ambitious loan-fuelled public works schemes of colonial treasurer Julius Vogel, the first round of which in 1871-4 saw the beginning of extensive railway construction (often in a piecemeal fashion dictated by the wealth and power of the regions). The development of provincial rugby unions closely follows the push of rail into the hinterland.

In just a few years, rugby had become a reason to travel, and some remarkable journeys were made, not least the first national tour embarked upon by an Auckland team in 1875, during which it lost every game.

I mean, to get from Auckland to Dunedin you had to go by sailing ship. You had to go out through the Manukau Harbour and over the Manukau bar. Sometimes you had to wait two or three days before the tides were right. It was quite an expedition. There was a sense of adventure about it, and it didn't happen often because of the time involved. It was something that players and people generally looked forward to.

Ron Palenski

Colonial Treasurer Julius Vogel in the 1860s. His loan-funded public works scheme built much of the infrastructure that allowed rugby to flourish.
Alexander Turnbull Library

. . . 'a game only worthy of savages' . . .

In a remarkably short time, then, rugby took hold in New Zealand, mirroring and eventually outliving the provincial boundaries as a patchwork of local loyalties. As the game spread, so did word of its vile influence on the corruptible souls of settler men. Rugby might well bring them together, it was said, but often to drink, gamble and fight on the side. Gambling had been central to the Victorian football culture of the West Coast since before rugby's arrival, so the new game was just another excuse for a wager. To the devotees of imperial ideology this was an affront to Victorian notions of games as moral improvement. If hard work was the proper path to wealth and godliness, they believed, then anything based on luck and chance was consequently sinful.

In 1877 a coroner described rugby as 'a game only worthy of savages', and the next year the *New Zealand Herald* was moved to thunder that 'bull-baiting and cock-fighting have more to commend them' than rugby. The Bank of New Zealand even announced that staff should not play 'the brutal and demoralising game of football'.

These were glimpses of the growing temperance movement, born out of a general fear from the 1880s on that the colony was becoming dangerously irreligious and morally corrupt. It was ironic, given rugby's origins as an aid to the inculcation of moral virtue in public schoolboys, but it was well founded. While rugby clubs multiplied in the years up to 1890, the churches were struggling to match that appeal, and the 1881 census showed 70 per cent of the population did not attend church regularly.

Maybe here the myth and reality converge again. The hard exigencies of eking a living from the settler economy produced a pragmatic, unsentimental merchant and working class, with more use for a good game of footy than a sermon. So much so that in 1883 the *Wairarapa Star* could advertise that, 'On Wednesday there will be a wet or dry practice, when every man with a sound constitution, good legs and a scorn for mutilation is expected to attend.'

Rugby writer Ron Palenski has described the now rapid sprouting of goal posts on muddy paddocks and city domains as 'a network of semaphore signals proclaiming an end to the various hybrids of football once played, and the beginning of the one true faith'. Rugby had completed its first great journey, from home to far away. From now on, the game and its adoptive home would grow up together.

HAKA

A winter's day dawns in central Hawke's Bay: limpid blue sky, frost on the grass, anticipation in the air. The annual first fifteen clash between Te Aute College and rival Maori boys college Tipene (or St Stephen's) from south of Auckland is more than just a school sports day. The whole district is aware of the game. The two colleges have a long history of intense rugby rivalry — so intense, in fact, that a fourth form exchange programme has been instigated for the week leading up to the match in an attempt to humanise the enemy.

The expressions of the boys before the game are as serious and focused as in any All Black changing-room. When the teams take the field, the Te Aute school haka is an awesome thing to behold. Tipene's response is equally fierce; right up in the Te Aute fifteen's faces, a challenge in the true sense. This is the modern expression of a bond between Maori culture and rugby that formed almost as soon as the game came to Aotearoa.

In the words of a forgotten master, quoted in the official school history, 'Football undoubtedly put Te Aute on the map.' Founded in 1854, Te Aute is an extraordinary blend of various colonial legacies. Over the past 120 years, Anglicanism, Maoritanga and rugby have combined to form a unique New Zealand institution. Conceived as a learning place for 'young Maori gentlemen', the original collection of classrooms and chapel was built on land donated by the local chief Te Hapuku for the purpose of educating the tribal children, and matched

. . . the Te Aute school haka is an awesome thing to behold.

The buildings of Te Aute College, where rugby helped to produce a breed of young Maori gentlemen who thought of England as home.
Hawke's Bay Cultural Trust, Hawke's Bay Museum

in acreage by the Governor, Sir George Grey, on the proviso that the school be open to all. Te Hapuku had earlier made the conscious decision that tribal land and forests be settled in partnership with the Pakeha, and it was through experiences like this that Grey formed his theory that indigenous people learned by example from white settlers, which he would later apply in South Africa.

It was a game that appealed to Maori people . . .

Te Aute quickly found a natural catchment area in the Hawke's Bay and East Coast as Maori families sent their chosen sons to be educated in a replica of the nineteenth century English boarding school. Famous old boys such as Apirana Ngata and Peter Buck consolidated Te Aute's reputation as a model of classical education. Writing of his first term there in 1897, Buck recalled, 'My neighbour in class scared the wits out of me by talking learnedly of Latin, Euclid and algebra, subjects which were beyond the curriculum of the village school in Taranaki which I had attended.'

Rugby was already the dominant sport by this time, and Buck goes on to describe Te Aute's style of play. 'We developed a game of our own by the wing forward dropping back from the scrum and playing as inside five-eighth. This was a departure from the orthodox game of two wing forwards and one five-eighth.' Such innovation was completely in keeping with the whole Maori approach to rugby. Something about the game appealed immensely, and Maori in turn made rugby more appealing to watch.

> It's a ball that has to be handled. And while there is room for individuality and individual success, it still depends on collaboration and cooperation. I think that group psyche, that togetherness, was something that appealed to Maori.
>
> *former Te Aute principal Brian Morris*

> It was a warrior sport. It was a game that appealed to Maori people because it was a team sport, it was something Maori people did together. They trained together for warfare in the days prior to rugby.
>
> *broadcaster Jim Perry*

> When you're dealing with Maori, you're dealing with whanau. And in those times, of course, families weren't made up of ones and twos, they were made up of sixes and sevens and tens. So you had a team! You had a competitive group.
>
> *former Race Relations Conciliator Hiwi Tauroa*

If the communal nature of rugby dovetailed with Maori social structure, based on whanau, hapu and iwi, the game also provided the colonisers with an ideal tool for indoctrination. By the 1880s, Maori were amongst the most ardent advocates of the game, including one pupil of Te Aute who defended it against accusations of brutality. 'It is essential and natural,' he said, 'for the young to indulge in some wholesome form of sport,' sounding every bit the middle-class Englishman.

> It became part and parcel of the whole colonisation process, the whole educational process. It wasn't an institution on its own, it became part of something else. So the way in which Maori were taught was one method, and along with that, to further entrench them into this system, they brought things like rugby.
>
> *television director Claudette Hauiti*

. . . Ellison's influence on rugby was and remains enormous.

If there is one person who embodies the cross-currents of imperialism, Maoridom and rugby, it is another of Te Aute's illustrious alumni, Thomas Rangiwahia Ellison — also known as Tamati Erihana. Born in 1867 at the small Maori settlement known as the Kaik on Otago Peninsula, Ellison's influence on rugby was and remains enormous.

Ellison attended Te Aute in the early 1880s where, he later wrote, 'my real introduction to the game took place'. As a boy, however, he had already been influenced by another great Maori player, his cousin, Jack Taiaroa, who scored nine tries in as many matches during an 1884 tour of Australia by the New Zealand team (he also set a national long jump record). Taiaroa, described by one

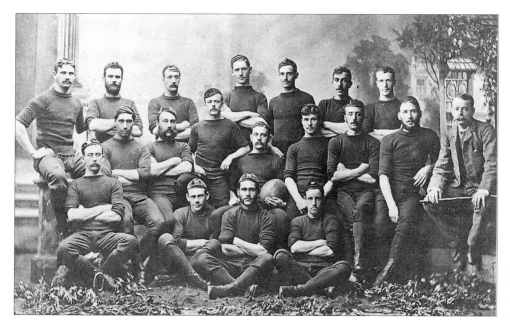

The New Zealand rugby team that toured Australia in 1884, including the great Jack Taiaroa (far left, middle row) and Joe Warbrick (second from right, front row).
Making New Zealand Collection, Alexander Turnbull Library

15

New South Wales newspaper as 'this prince of footballers', was the son of Hori Kerei Taiaroa (Ellison's uncle), one of the first Maori to enter parliament after the establishment of Maori seats in 1867 (when the Pakeha population overtook Maori). Representing Southern Maori, he waged a lonely campaign to bring Ngai Tahu land claims to the attention of the European administration. His preference for parliamentary channels of redress brought him into conflict with other Ngai Tahu when, in protest over broken promises made during the land deals, they built a village on a large sheep station in 1877. Taiaroa was caught between his sure knowledge that his people were right in their claim, and his belief that such means would not achieve their ends.

While the young Tom Ellison was growing up and going to Te Aute, a succession of major hui took place around the North Island to discuss breaches of the Treaty of Waitangi, and two Maori delegations went to London to appeal directly to the British Crown. Such was the world in which Maori were steadily becoming masters of a game invented by their British overlords.

Having made a name for himself playing for the Poneke Club in Wellington, Ellison embarked on his own historic journey. In 1888 the first tour of Britain by a New Zealand sports team took place. What became known as the Natives

The New Zealand Native Football Team that toured Britain in 1888, one of the most extraordinary journeys undertaken by a sporting team in any code.
Making New Zealand Collection, Turnbull Library

Tour was a mammoth rugby trip, lasting over a year, involving 107 matches in Britain and Australia and taking an enormous toll on the players. Ellison, who played forward in more than 80 of the games, died aged only 37 — some believe as a result of the physical punishment he suffered on the tour. By tour's end the Natives were said to be the only team to have ever limped onto the field.

The Natives Team was the brainchild of two quite different men, Joe Warbrick, a leading Maori rugby player and contemporary of Taiaroa who played in the 1884 tour of New South Wales, and Tom Eyton, an English-born veteran of the Taranaki land wars. Warbrick seems to have conceived of the tour while planning a more modest game between a Maori team and the visiting British team of 1888. At the same time, Eyton had formed the idea that a Maori tour of Britain could be not only a sporting success, but a financial one too. Twenty-one of the 26 players in the touring party had Maori blood in them, including three of Joe Warbrick's brothers and three brothers from another great Maori rugby family, the Wynyards. The inclusion of European players saw the team's title changed from New Zealand Maori to New Zealand Native, since all were said to have been born in the colony.

The fact that at least two players were Australian or British-born was probably known to Warbrick and Eyton, but to admit as much would have compromised the commercial aims of the tour. In the event, the racial composition of the team was not a major talking point in Britain, where the interest was more in the perceived benefits of fostering imperial links with such ventures. Such a view would have been supported by the fact that the Maori players were by no means representative of the general Maori population in the 1880s. Most had gone through the European school system — six from Te Aute College alone — and several spoke about the tour as 'going home'.

The haka was performed right from the beginning of the tour . . .

> For a lot of English people in the 1880s, their view of Maori tended to be of tough, frankly savage, men, who'd fought in the land wars. The view was very narrow. And of course, when the Maoris actually arrived in some of these small towns they wore top hats and spoke very good English, and talked about being home. But at the same time these Maori men had a belief in their own culture. They wanted to take some of their culture with them to England, so to some extent they lived in both worlds. The haka was performed right from the beginning of the tour, and the Australian crowds were very enthusiastic — although there were reports that some of the female spectators were overwhelmed by the passion of it!
>
> *historian Eamon Bolger*

17

Tom Ellison, captain of the Natives Team, in whose all-too-brief life came together various strands of Maori, European and rugby history.
NZ Rugby Museum

The haka's reception at the first British game was different. The team wore what was described as traditional Maori dress, to the astonishment of the crowd and negative comment in the press. From then on the Natives avoided wearing costumes before games, but persevered with the haka. When crowds began turning up to see the Maori arrive at railway stations, however, the team did occasionally dress up (in one instance with black masks to amuse the throng).

One of the youngest players in the Native Team was 18-year-old Wiri Nehua, selected for the tour while still at Te Aute. Nehua played in only eight of the British matches, but his contribution is still remarkable for a diary he kept of the entire tour. Elegantly handwritten in Maori, the diary records much detail of travel and matches, but also reveals the mind of its author and the dual worlds he inhabited. On the ship to England, Nehua writes knowledgeably about the Red Sea and its place in the Old Testament, the eruption of Vesuvius, the birthplace of Napoleon Bonaparte and the British fort on Gibraltar. Once in England, Nehua records the players' penchant for walking out in the evenings and visiting local theatres and music halls for entertainment. He notes that members of the team were mistaken for American Indians, probably because Buffalo Bill's travelling circus was in town at the same time.

Nehua's diary also shows that the Native players, while educated in the manner of English gentlemen, showed a distinct empathy for the lower classes in Britain, and an awareness of the class system in general. This is borne out by the very different attitudes encountered by the team in different parts of England. The London press and the English Rugby Football Union tended to be critical of the Natives' allegedly rough playing style, whereas in the north of England (where the standard of football was altogether higher) the team was generally praised for its competitiveness. These were the early manifestations of a philosophical split within British rugby, between the southern guardians of the amateur ethic and the northern champions of professionalism. Eventually this would lead to the breakaway of the northern unions in 1895, which was the beginning of the rival (and professional) code of rugby league. As historian Greg Ryan states, 'That the colonial visitors came to identify with the recalcitrants in this division raises doubts as to the extent to which public school old boys who took the basic rules of games to the frontiers of Empire were able to reinforce this with their accompanying ethos.'

No one exemplifies this better than Tom Ellison, who on his return from the tour wrote a seminal book, *The Art of Rugby Football*, in which he argued for the

. . . tended to be critical of the Natives' allegedly rough playing style . . .

compensation of players, and pointed out the ludicrous imposition of asking working men to sacrifice earnings for a game that people paid to watch. 'Getting the best men away without giving them some allowance above their actual hotel and travelling expenses,' wrote Ellison, '. . . would be obviously unfair and tantamount to prohibiting them from going away at all.'

Such sentiments were not just a hundred years ahead of their time, but would have been verging on blasphemy to an English Union convinced of the higher moral quality of amateur sport. But then Ellison was ahead of his time in many ways. Believed to be the first Maori admitted to the Bar, he would also take up his uncle's cause on behalf of Ngai Tahu, standing three times, unsuccessfully, for parliament. In 1892 he was instrumental in defending the newly-formed New Zealand Rugby Football Union from the regional ambitions of the rebel unions of Otago, Canterbury and Southland. The next year he captained the New Zealand team that toured Australia. He invented the position of wing forward that would be a successful and controversial feature of New Zealand rugby for decades to come. And it was Ellison who proposed that New Zealand's national team should wear the black jersey and silver fern — just as the Natives had.

Towards the turn of the century, a rugby team embarks on an away trip from Nelson to Richmond.
Tyree Collection, Nelson Provincial Museum

William Pember Reeves, whose early labour legislation would begin the gradual enshrinement of Saturday as New Zealand's day of leisure – and rugby.
Alexander Turnbull Library

One was war and the other was rugby.

> If Tom Ellison was living in the 1990s instead of the 1890s he'd be Sir Tom Ellison and he'd be revered as one of the great New Zealanders.
>
> *Ron Palenski*

Tom Ellison lived on the cusp of two eras. By the end of the 1880s, New Zealand was moving out of its initial phase of European settlement and into a period of consolidation and assertion of a colonial identity. A decade of economic depression had dented the settlers' initial optimism; opportunities for those without capital or land were harder to find, and new ideas about the role of government were emerging. The 1890s saw attempts to break up large estates and put small farmers onto the land, and in the towns the beginnings of the labour movement found a champion in William Pember Reeves, whose legislation would regulate employment and impose compulsory half-day closing on all shops — making rugby easier to play in the process. As wool prices rose and meat and dairy exports grew with the advent of refrigeration, the wealth and political influence of small farmers began to increase.

Money, leisure time and better transport entrenched rugby's already strong presence. Grandstands began to appear next to grounds. Liberal Party politicians, the friends of the farmer, fostered and exploited the new prosperity, and none more ruthlessly than Richard John Seddon, the tough ex-publican from the West Coast goldfields who assumed premiership in 1893. Seddon arrived in power in time to shape the country's transition from frontier society to colonial nationhood. He would find two perfect vehicles for asserting New Zealand's place in the great scheme of Empire. One was war, and the other was rugby.

SONS OF EMPIRE

Ironically, the first real glimmerings of New Zealand nationalism were part of a wider effort to demonstrate solidarity with imperial Britain. By staking a claim on the fields of Empire, New Zealand began to find and proclaim an identity of its own. At the turn of the century, when Britain went to war in South Africa against the Dutch Afrikaaner settlers, Seddon grabbed the opportunity to impress Mother England with her colony's loyalty. It was, said the Premier, 'our bounden duty to support the Empire and to assist in every way the Imperial authorities whenever occasion demands'. In October 1899 the first of ten volunteer contingents left for the Boer War, farewelled by a large and enthusiastically patriotic crowd on Jervois Quay in Wellington.

> We wanted to be first away, we wanted to be first to offer forces, and we were! Seddon was the first to offer a contingent to South Africa, and that was picked up by the general population. And any voices of dissent were drowned because they were very minor. And it was seen as an adventure. Because the veterans of the New Zealand land wars, which was our only experience of war to that date, were the same age as the Second World War veterans are today. So it was almost a competition within the Empire to prove ourselves as loyal sons.
>
> *military historian Chris Pugsley*

Ellison had already made the connection, in his *Art of Rugby Football*, that 'rugby is a soldier-making game'. A direct echo of the public school ethos that Waterloo had been won on the playing fields of Eton, perhaps, but given a pragmatic edge in the New Zealand context. By this time the colonial approach to rugby was to place winning as high or higher than merely participating as an objective of the game. The New Zealand soldiers in South Africa impressed the British with their fighting, and were regarded by some as the best mounted troops in the war. Again, as historian Jock Phillips has noted, the fact that the proportion of New

We wanted to be first away, we wanted to be first to offer forces, and we were!

New Zealand troops in South Africa for the Boer War — eager volunteers at the forefront of Empire.
Boer War Scrapbook, Alexander Turnbull Library

Zealand troops drawn from rural or manual occupations pretty much matched their percentage of the general population — well below half — did nothing to dispel 'the image of this as an army of frontier farmers'.

New Zealanders at home made the link between war and rugby almost automatically, and were extremely proud that war heroes such as Lieutenant William Hardham were also rugby men. A blacksmith by trade, Hardham won the Victoria Cross for rescuing a wounded comrade under fire, and the newspapers were quick to point out that he was a player as well as a warrior.

> For a small country, starting to be noticed on the battlefields of Empire was very important. To that extent, rugby became a superb training ground for making New Zealanders the territorials of the Empire, which is really the way we defined ourselves from about the turn of the century through to 1950 or thereabouts. Rugby was at the very cutting edge of national identity and it was at the cutting edge of the way we saw our mission in the world.
> *historian Jock Phillips*

Dave Gallaher in Boer War uniform, soon to be hero of peace as well as war.
NZ Rugby Museum

Among the New Zealand volunteers was a 28-year-old rugby player named Dave Gallaher. Born in Ulster but raised in New Zealand, he was the epitome of the new New Zealander; six feet tall, strong, silent, taciturn even — but gallant, self-reliant, modest and gentlemanly. Gallaher had played club rugby for Ponsonby and had represented Auckland before leaving for South Africa, where he served as a corporal in the 6th Contingent in 1901. Here he would have been among those stout New Zealand men, now calling themselves 'Kiwis' and 'Maorilanders', who so impressed an imperial officer class that was fretting about the physical and moral state of the British male.

> The interesting thing was that New Zealanders often don't know who they are until people overseas tell them. And in the Boer War the British became very concerned with the fact that a very high proportion of recruits going into the British Army were turned away because they were physically not up to it. And a great theory began to build up in England that the British race and the Anglo-Saxon race were in decline.

Suddenly the British looked at the New Zealanders in South Africa and said, 'Here are these enormous, tough colonial men; they are the great hope of Empire!' And so New Zealanders began to think of themselves as much more physically strong than men in England.

Jock Phillips

I think the Boer War more than any other war was seen as a triumph of Empire. The New Zealanders went away for 12 months, they went off as heroes, fêted at the wharves, and they came back to the same sort of reception. In a sense this was the first overseas tour that New Zealand had been allowed to play on an imperial stage.

Chris Pugsley

Dave Gallaher, All Black captain.
NZ Rugby Museum

The British view of colonial colossi (and the willing New Zealand acceptance of that view) was reinforced very soon after the Boer War when a British rugby team visited in 1904. Captained by one D R Beddell-Sivright, the tourists were roundly thrashed by the colonials in front of massive crowds, including one game at Wellington's Athletic Park before 23,000 spectators — nearly a third of the city's population at the time. Despite the hiding, the British formed a patronising view of their rivals, with Beddell-Sivright predicting that a New Zealand team would never win an international in Britain. He could not have been more wrong.

The following year the first official All Black team left New Zealand on the first official tour of Britain. Captained by Dave Gallaher, Boer War veteran and outstanding wing forward, the so-called 'Originals' would stun and excite the British public and cause unprecedented jubilation in New Zealand. As in war, their object was not just victory, but to show the imperial mother that her sons were worthy. They were, in the words of Seddon, 'missionaries of Empire'.

THE ORIGINALS

From its inception, the 1905 tour was as much a political as a sporting venture — at least in the minds of men like Seddon. Before the team left, New Zealanders were largely indifferent and no great crowds gathered to farewell the players. On the other hand, the Premier, his deputy Joseph Ward and opposition leader William Massey were all there. Seddon saw the tour as another perfect opportunity to 'draw the colony closer to the Mother Country', in the words of one contemporary chronicle. In consultation with Massey, Seddon had arranged for William Pember Reeves, now High Commissioner in London, to report back to New Zealand on the tour's progress.

23

The Originals of 1905, including vice-captain Billy Stead (third from left, middle row) and Bob Deans, scorer of the famously disputed try against Wales (far right, front row).
W J Wallace Collection, Alexander Turnbull Library

. . . Seddon was happy to fan the flames.

The 27 players themselves were no doubt more concerned with the peculiar demands of touring at the start of the twentieth century. More than a month at sea each way, with four months of rugby in between, this was to set the standard for rugby tours to come. If early English predictions that the All Blacks would not prosper were confounded by their initial 55-4 drubbing of Devon, the British press was divided on the quality of the team. At the heart of most criticism was the use of the wing forward position (played by Gallaher) — Tom Ellison's invention — which some commentators felt was tantamount to cheating. They argued for the rigorous application of the offside laws, and this, combined with continued carping about the position, made the tour something of a misery for the stoic Gallaher. Like the Natives before them, the Originals were encountering that very British resistance to a perceived win-at-all-costs antipodean philosophy.

Nevertheless, as the tour progressed and the victory count mounted, criticism turned to praise and admiration, and the crowds at matches began to grow. Back in New Zealand public interest in the team's fortunes had ignited, and Seddon was happy to fan the flames. Official cablegrams from Reeves were quickly relayed to the enthralled nation.

The newspapers were only published on Saturdays and Monday mornings. My father lived in Wanganui, and each Sunday morning as a matter of duty, half the males in the town above the age of 15 went to the Post Office where at about 8.30 or nine o'clock — the news had been coming through by telegraph — the scores of the match were put up.

T P McLean

Analysis of the tour took on the tone of an extended hymn to the virtues of life in the distant colony. When the *London Daily Mail* asked Seddon to describe the reaction at home to the All Blacks' success, he replied in characteristic style: 'The natural and healthy conditions of colonial life produce stalwart and athletic sons of whom New Zealand and the Empire are justly proud.' In England, Reeves was doing much the same, claiming the All Blacks were the beneficiaries of the 'vaster opportunities' of the colonial way of life, including a climate 'brisk, breezy and bracing with a combination of sea and mountain air'.

Seddon even drew a comparison between the brave boys of rugby and the revered veterans of the Boer War, when he told the *Daily Mail* that news of the tour was awaited almost as eagerly as had been news from the South African front. This was seen in some quarters as demeaning of the veterans, but as historian Len Richardson makes clear, Seddon's point was to place the All Blacks in a continuum of imperial allegiance.

New Zealanders think that rugby and politics were separate for 50 years or thereabouts until 1981. In fact, rugby and politics have been intimately intertwined in New Zealand from the very beginning, and particularly in 1905.

Jock Phillips

Seddon's ambitions — he was also facing an election — were surprisingly complemented by certain attitudes in Britain at the time. The concerns about British virility already evident during the Boer War had developed into full-blown theories. While the All Blacks demolished everything put in front of them, a minor cult classic entitled *The Decline and Fall of the British Empire* was circulating among the upper classes. Written by a young Oxford graduate, the pamphlet argued that advanced social decay would soon be the ruin of the greatest empire the world had seen. Such fears were encouraged by the 1905 defeat of the Russian navy by the Japanese, and corresponding alarm that the world's population was shifting in favour of Africa and Asia. So the simple game of rugby became a vessel for the hopes and dreams of imperialists, both in Britain and New Zealand.

. . . the simple game of rugby became a vessel for the hopes and dreams of imperialists . . .

25

They sang the whole day! Well, of course, the Welsh sing all the time, don't they really?

As historian Timothy Buchanan has written, 'The rugby players were not simply colonial heroes or missionaries of Empire, but testimony to white supremacy. Racial purity [Seddon] argued, must be safeguarded so that the Empire would be ready if needed to resist the Asiatic hordes.'

For all Seddon's posturing, these ambassadors of racial purity were a typically mixed New Zealand team. Among them was vice-captain Billy Stead, a part-Maori from Southland who, as a boy, had carried Tom Ellison's boots when the great man trained. After the tour Stead would write a book (with Gallaher), *The Complete Rugby Footballer*, 270 pages long, written in three weeks and as important as Ellison's earlier work. By 1905, the Maori contribution to rugby was an integral part of the New Zealand game, including the haka, performed before every game of the tour. At the final test against Wales, the Welsh Football Union agreed to a musical reply, and so another tradition was born. The sound of 40,000 Welshmen singing the chorus to their anthem 'Land of my Fathers' was 'the most impressive incident I have ever witnessed on a football field', wrote the *Lyttelton Times* reporter. 'It gave a semi-religious solemnity to this memorable contest.'

The 1905 All Blacks crush Middlesex at Stamford Bridge.
Hocken Library

5.
On the gymnasium floor, jerseys await their owners, the Te Aute College first fifteen, before their match with fellow Maori school Tipene, or St Stephen's. At Te Aute, like Tipene, Maoritanga, rugby and the peculiarities of an English boarding school tradition have grown around each other for more than a century.

6.
More than just a school game, the Te Aute-Tipene clash is a drawcard throughout the central Hawke's Bay.

7.
The tree-lined drive, the leafy winter field — it could be the historical birthplace of rugby, but for the faces in the crowd and on the ground.

8.
Despite a rivalry so fierce that a fourth-form exchange programme between Te Aute and Tipene has been started in the week before the big game, an effort to humanise the enemy, both victor and vanquished find honour in their efforts. The aftermatch haka articulates, far better than words can, the age-old bond between Maori and rugby.

Dad often used to talk about the singing that went on all day from the hotel attached to the rugby ground, and he said that by the time the players went on they were all worked up. Six o'clock in the morning they started. It was right adjacent to the rugby ground and the rugby players could hear them, you see. They sang the whole day! Well, of course, the Welsh sing all the time, don't they really?

Billy Stead's daughter Florence Wilson

All Black E E Booth writes home during the English leg of the tour.
NZ Herald

The Welsh test also gave rugby one of its most enduring talking points, in the form of the All Black three-quarter Bob Deans' disputed try — the try that would have prevented the team's only loss of the tour. Deans himself telegramed the *Daily Mail* to avow the disallowed try had indeed been scored, claiming he was pulled back from the line by the time the Scottish referee John Dallas (wearing street clothes) arrived. Billy Stead, who didn't play due to illness, stood in as line umpire that day, and always swore the try was valid.

He saw it – he was line umpire. He saw it scored! He objected and all the rest of it. The referee was half way down the field when he went over, and by the time he got up there they'd pulled him back, you see.

Florence Wilson

My father was talking to a man called Owens, a Welshman who had settled in New Zealand some years before, who was saying to old Jack McLean that he hoped the All Blacks would win and carry on with their winning ways, because he was now well settled in this country and he wanted New Zealand to be the winners. Well the telegraph boy came out and put up the score — New Zealand nil, Wales three — and according to Jack McLean, Taffy Owens flung his hat as far up in the air as he possibly could and raced up the Wanganui Avenue and wasn't seen for days, most of which were spent in a total state of drunkenness.

It could be said that in every church service for years and years after, the first prayer was: Our father which art in heaven, please make sure that John Dallas be killed in the most violent way because of the decision that robbed Bobby Deans of the try, which would have squared the game and given Billy Wallace the chance to kick the goal which infallibly he would have kicked and the tour would have been unbeaten. Amen.

T P McLean

Seddon lost no time in capitalising on the nation's shock at the loss, asking questions in parliament and making patronising references to the disputed try being the most interesting thing to have happened to Wales in years. In Australia, where Seddon's shameless lobbying for imperial honours was viewed with greater clarity and some distaste, the *Bulletin* reported the defeat gleefully:

Seddon's brash appropriation of
the All Blacks' success was not
lost on everyone.
NZ Herald

The gloom that is hanging over Maoriland at time of writing is not, as might be supposed by its density, due to volcanic disturbances, but to the fact that the world's record tour has had its symmetry spoiled by a crowd of prancing Taffies.

The team was rewarded for its magnificent feat with a trip home through North America, paid for by the government. What became known as the 'American holiday' was another chance to fly the New Zealand flag abroad. The All Blacks played several exhibition matches, and the tour coincided with a low point in the history of American college football, which was under attack for its brutality. At the All Blacks' first match in New York, played on a baseball ground, the small crowd included several college professors interested in reforming the local game, and particularly the dangerous practice of scoring with a 'flying wedge' (a V-shaped formation of players charging at the opposition). Once again, there were ethnic undertones to this semi-evangelistic leg of the tour.

This was all bound up with the idea that the United States, England and the colonies represented the great hope of the Anglo-Saxon race, and that we could show our Anglo-Saxon kith and kin in the United States that we had these great frontier heroes.

Jock Phillips

Seddon was roundly criticised for squandering money on the holiday that might otherwise have gone toward much-needed public works. 'Seddon knows no laws,' thundered the *Christchurch Truth*, 'he is a law unto himself.' By the time the team arrived back in New Zealand in March 1906, New Zealanders were used to calling the Premier the 'minister of football'. A crowd of about 12,000 gathered at the Auckland wharf to watch the *Sonoma* dock, and to witness Seddon, who had already boarded the ship with the pilot, lead the conquering heroes down the gangway. If his antics were regarded with some cynicism by various commentators, the achievements of the All Blacks were not belittled in the process. 'The laurels so worthy and honourably won by the team,' sang the *Auckland Star*, 'were now the property of the people of the colony.'

In England, the team had become the object of almost lyrical praise. 'When Shakespeare wrote to the effect that England never did nor never should lie at the proud foot of a conqueror,' proclaimed the *Daily News*, 'he evidently overlooked the possibility of a team of New Zealand footballers invading this land at some time or other.'

The Originals were even celebrated in a song, sung by Zena Dare, the beautiful Edwardian actress and singer, who starred in a forgotten 1906 musical, *The Little Cherub*. In what was described as the 'tomboy number', the female cast acted out a pantomime of male sports that included rugby and mentioned the previous year's All Blacks. The song was called 'I should so love to be a boy', and ended with Miss Dare kicking a football into the auditorium.

The triumphant return of these 'missionaries of Empire' seemed to confirm an image of New Zealanders as stout frontier men and women, British to the core but with healthy minds and constitutions, born of mountain air and honest outdoor work. Yet this was far from the truth as the new century advanced. The bands of footloose men that once roamed the land clearing scrub, felling trees and building railroads were disappearing. New Zealand was rapidly becoming an urban, regulated, settled nation of shopkeepers and office workers.

Zena Dare, star of the London stage, who sang of the All Blacks' exploits after their victorious tour.
Peter Downes Collection

Rugby, I think, was a very good trainer because it provided a model of how to work as a team. It provided a structured environment. You worked like mad together and at the blow of a whistle you stopped, just like in a factory. And you learnt that if you worked together you were more successful than if you worked as individuals.

Jock Phillips

. . . it provided a model of how to work as a team.

ALL WORK AND NO PAY

If rugby had become one of Mother England's apron strings and a means of articulating a new colonial identity, it was also beginning to show up certain subtle differences in attitudes between home and away. The public school ethos had not translated perfectly to New Zealand, where a tougher terrain and the absence of the leisured middle and upper classes had demanded different things of players — not least a stolidly practical approach to simply getting a game up. As Tom Ellison had already noted, there was a vast difference between popping down to the local ground in Surrey or Warwickshire, and scrabbling together a team of working men and transporting them many miles on rough roads to the game.

Rugby, of course, was still a relatively young code, and the other ball game spreading rapidly throughout Britain — Association Football, or soccer — was already turning professional as gate takings were passed on to players. Rugby was popular in all the areas soccer was, and particularly keenly played by mining communities in the northern industrial counties. As the top players became local heroes and public demand for their performances grew, so did the recognition that money had a place in this game; how else to ensure that miners and factory workers made themselves available to play, so ensuring a good gate? Soon clubs were illicitly paying individual players to retain their membership, and inducements to switch clubs were being offered.

An artist's depiction of the All Blacks' 15-0 defeat of England at Crystal Palace in 1905.
NZ Rugby Union

In 1893 Yorkshire was the first rugby county to openly suggest that players be compensated for loss of working time, which was strongly opposed by the southern English clubs. A meeting of the Rugby Football Union voted to oppose what was considered the thin end of the professional wedge, and two years later in 1895 the northern clubs of Yorkshire, Lancashire and Cheshire broke away to form the Northern Football Union. This would ultimately become the Rugby League, organising play on a club rather than a county basis. It was a huge blow to the Rugby Union, since the northern clubs were generally the strongest. (Indeed, one can argue that the 1905 All Blacks were not playing the cream of English football, though this is not to say the Originals didn't revolutionise the game on their triumphant tour.)

New Zealanders, with their peculiarly pragmatic and unsentimental approach to rugby, often found more in common with the men of the north, whose working lives would have more clearly matched their own. The 1888 Natives were treated more as an honest sporting rival in the north than as a novelty or some kind of imperial bridge-builder as they were in the south. And the speculative nature of the tour was, of course, frowned upon by the guardians of amateurism. Earlier in the same year as the Natives tour, the English Union refused to officially sanction the tour of New Zealand by an English team due to the perception that it was more to benefit the promoters than to spread the good word of rugby.

The 1905 All Blacks encountered the same bias, though for slightly complex reasons. Before the tour the cash-strapped New Zealand Union had sought financial guarantees from the British unions and counties. Scotland, having lost heavily with a similar scheme during a Canadian tour in 1904, declined, but promised the New Zealanders the entire gate minus expenses. By the time the All Blacks reached Scotland the tour had reached fever pitch and, much to the dismay of the Scots, the gate was unusually large. Disgruntled, the dour amateurists of Edinburgh also needled the All Blacks for their daily three-shilling allowance, dubbing them 'three bob a day men'.

English misgivings about antipodean attitudes to amateurism were given further credence when, only two years after the 1905 tour, four of the Originals turned up in a rugby league team touring Britain. They had seen league being played in the north and felt no disloyalty or dishonour in giving it a go. Assembled in New Zealand using private money by a young entrepreneur, A H Baskerville, the team also contained four new All Blacks and a number of top provincial players (including Lance Todd, who later signed for Wigan and became a league

. . . in fact they didn't get paid very much at all. Some of them didn't get paid at all.

The so-called All Golds, New Zealand's first rugby league team, that so incensed the amateurists of English rugby in 1907.
Auckland Rugby League Collection, Alexander Turnbull Library

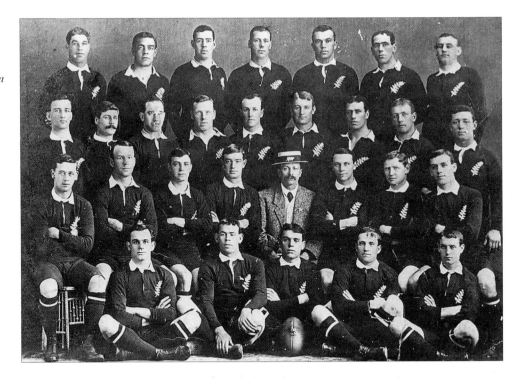

commentator for the BBC). The New Zealanders became known as the 'All Golds', and were responsible for the advent of league in New Zealand, and in New South Wales, where several games were played on the way home.

> They were called the All Golds rather derisively because of the imagined amount of money they were getting, but in fact they didn't get paid very much at all. Some of them didn't get paid at all.
>
> *Ron Palenski*

> It looked as if these colonials were coming back to Britain where there was this huge potential market for spectators, and milking the system for all its worth, by getting their share of the gate and running home to the colonies with the money.
>
> *Len Richardson*

So strong was the resentment in amateur British circles, and so real was the threat from league, that a team and a tour were organised in 1908 to put the wayward New Zealanders back on the right rugby path. It wasn't just the question of money, but professionalism in its broadest sense — training too hard, taking winning too seriously — that bothered the keepers of the flame. Called the Anglo-Welsh team due to the refusal of Scotland or Ireland to even bother with the recalcitrant colonials, the team's objectives were somewhat obscured by

. . . responsible for a minor rugby dynasty . . .

the thumping received at the hands of the All Blacks (apart from one drawn test when New Zealand blooded several new players).

Oddly enough, the paranoia over league that inspired the Anglo-Welsh tour was directly responsible for a minor rugby dynasty in New Zealand. Syd Jackson, best known to New Zealanders as a proponent of Maori sovereignty, is the son of the great Maori player and 1930s All Black, Everard Jackson, and the grandson of one of the Anglo-Welsh players, F S Jackson. When an English newspaper claimed he had signed to play league at the end of the tour, Jackson was summarily dismissed on the Australian leg.

> He wasn't asked whether or not that was correct. He was quite literally thrown out onto the street in Australia to fend for himself as best he could. And eventually he ended up on the East Coast [of the North Island] somehow, and married our grandmother.
>
> *Syd Jackson*

There was resistance to this imperial lecturing too, with factions inside New Zealand and Australian rugby even considering a breakaway Southern Federation of Rugby that would have included California (capitalising on the moves there to clean up college football). More players defected to the professional code and a network of provincial leagues was established throughout the country. But the battle for rugby's amateur soul would not be settled by sporting committees and rebel players. It would be settled by war.

THE GREATER GAME

When Britain went to war with Germany in 1914, New Zealand followed automatically. Of the 100,000 New Zealand troops who served overseas, nearly 17,000 were killed and another 45,000 wounded — horrendous statistics by any standard. But New Zealanders seemed unusually prepared for this level of sacrifice; even after the disastrous nine-month campaign at Gallipoli no detectable anti-war sentiment could be heard through the patriotic clamour at home.

The war was, in fact, the culmination of a period of peacetime militarism during which school cadets were established and compulsory military training introduced. All this was parallel to the consolidation of rugby as the national game, and its appropriation by imperial-minded New Zealanders as a bulwark against racial and moral decline. The country may have been proclaimed a Dominion in 1907, but the old colonial connection was not diminished. When

It would be settled by war.

the Imperial Commander-in-Chief, Lord Kitchener, visited in 1910, the bonds of Empire were again celebrated. 'It proclaims that the Empire is one,' wrote one observer, 'not only in sentiment, but in discipline, organisation, armament, equipment and the command of Imperial troops.'

Rugby had been seen as the 'soldier-making game' since before the Boer War. Along with other sporting codes it became a logical recruiting ground when, in the words of the Te Aute College history, 'the British Empire was jeopardised by the marching feet of the Huns'. War became 'the greater game' for which all stern men had been well prepared. When the MP for Gisborne, Sir James Carroll, spoke at the farewell of Maori reinforcements in 1915, he said: 'The lads from beneath the Southern Cross are fighting shoulder to shoulder on the Gallipoli Peninsula, and many of them are better soldiers because of the mock battles they have fought on the football field.'

> Rugby had been seen as the 'soldier-making game' since before the Boer War.

Entire teams and clubs signed up together, often becoming part of the same battalion, and often dying together in the same wasteland of mud and barbed wire. Rugby became a metaphor for battle. As one wartime commentator wrote, 'when the New Zealand boys — the forwards at the Dardanelles or in France — took new ground from the foe, their scrum was never pushed back'. At first, the motivation was adventure. The first members of the New Zealand Expeditionary Force to depart, writes Chris Pugsley, 'sailed not as New Zealanders but rather as a number of highly competitive provincial teams: Otago, Canterbury,

Wellington and Auckland. Jealous of their reputation, more conscious of their differences than of any national identity, they were sailing overseas to play a series of games whose results, in their minds, were preordained. The British Empire would win. The only real concern was that they . . . would not arrive in time for the competition.'

> After the 1915 casualty lists started to come in, which was a few months after the Gallipoli invasion, it became much more difficult to consider the war as a game, although that terminology crops up often in the letters that people were sending home or the things that were being written during the war. Certainly by 1917 and 1918 the incidence of that description is getting much lower. People are beginning to deal with the consequences of large numbers of people dying, large numbers of people being very badly wounded. And the fact that it was very difficult to continue functioning, both financially and morally, from the First World War.
>
> *historian Fiona Hall*

Writing of the Gallipoli landings from his hospital bed in Cairo, Private Kohi Hemana observed that, 'It is just like football . . . The boys were very fit, good enough to win any match of football.' Another wrote that, 'there is not a man who has disgraced the old Christchurch Football Club. They died as heroes, every one.' And another wrote to the father of his dead comrade, 'I knew Roy very well as he was captain of our Auckland Battalion rugby team and I played half in this team in Egypt . . . Your son met his death in a gallant manner as befits a New Zealander and a man, and I hope that the fact that he played the game to

Rugby became a metaphor for battle.

The Wellington Battalion rugby team in Egypt, 1915, part of an army that sailed 'not as New Zealanders, but rather as a number of highly competitive provincial teams'.
B H Morrison Collection, QEII Army Memorial Museum

*. . . a morale-
booster for the
troops . . .*

the bitter end will be a great source of satisfaction to you.'

Throughout the war, New Zealand soldiers played rugby. One of the first things the Expeditionary Force did was form company teams to contest the battalion championships, and provincial teams to play for brigade honours. In Palestine the Mounted Rifles played a seven-a-side competition lasting the entire war, finally won by the Auckland Mounted Rifles (who received a £100 prize).

> Right throughout you're conscious that, as they say, the worst fights in the schoolyard are between brothers. So it was with the rugby — the broken bones, the broken ribs. The province came first . . . It became structured as part of the deliberate competitiveness that the New Zealand commanders wanted to encourage. And in the same way that New Zealanders don't fight to play the game, they fight to win, so they played rugby.
>
> *Chris Pugsley*

The New Zealand Division was commanded by Major-General Andrew Russell, a Sandhurst-trained Hawke's Bay farmer. The archetypal imperial colonial gentleman, he used rugby as a morale-booster for the troops, forming the Divisional All Blacks from the best players to be found among the ranks.

King George V presents the King's Cup to New Zealand after the British Empire championship at war's end.
QEII Army Memorial Museum

He asked his selectors to look for former All Blacks, North and South Island reps and the top provincial players, pulling them back into the training depot. They were trained in physical fitness, bayonet fighting and bombing, and were kept together and fed up and fattened until the end of the rugby season. And one was conscious that if the war had ended before the rugby season, then perhaps they would still have been there.

Chris Pugsley

Russell wanted the New Zealand Division to be the best performed arm of the allied army, and that included rugby. Two All Black teams were formed, one from troops in France, known as the Trench team, and one from the troops in Britain. They had mixed fortunes in their matches against other national teams, and it was always the ambition of the New Zealanders to form one team from the two and beat all-comers. The King's Cup, a final competition to decide the best team among the allied nations, was their chance to do that. And with the exception of a loss to Australia in the round robin, the New Zealand Army team lived up to Russell's expectations, beating England (designated 'Mother Country' in the official programme) in the final at Twickenham. The presentation of the trophy by King George V largely symbolised the achievement of the New Zealand team and Division. As Jock Phillips states, 'few people outside of Britain have heard of Twickenham, or even of Gallipoli . . . New Zealand's male triumphs did not win attention in the eyes of the world but merely in the eyes of the British ruling class.'

Among those who made the ultimate sacrifice for God, King and country was Dave Gallaher, captain of the great 1905 All Blacks, killed at Passchendaele during the third battle of Ypres in October 1917. A hero of war and peace, he would later be remembered as one who 'bore himself in the days of the Empire's crucial test as he had done on the rugby field'.

The wasteful carnage of the First World War meant that rugby, like most male sports, emerged in tatters; so many young men dead, injured or psychologically damaged; no fees paid for so long that clubs struggled for years to regain their pre-war strength. There would have been little fight left for the right to play rugby the New Zealand way — even if the argument had survived the war. In fact, the war effectively ended the philosophical tug-of-war between strict amateurism and a very mild form of professionalism. For most of the century the New Zealand Rugby Football Union would obey the laws set down in England by the inheritors of an élite tradition.

37

. . . there is this rush to get back on to the playing fields as quickly as they can . . .

It gave scope for those people who believed that the playing fields were where you inculcated certain values and prepared people for the defence of Empire, to actually say that that is what happened. So when the war ends, there is this rush to get back on to the playing fields as quickly as they can to celebrate, in effect, the victory on the battlefields.

Len Richardson

Rugby finally succumbed to the pressures of a relentlessly commercial world in the mid-1990s, the last major sporting code to pay players for their time and skill.

When the All Blacks played the Wallabies in the second Bledisloe Cup test in 1995, the rituals of New Zealand rugby were played out as they had been since the game caught the collective imagination. At after-match functions all over the country, friend and foe, victor and vanquished sat down together to unite in their support of the national team. Unity out of diversity. But it was the end of an era, for better or worse. The last amateur game of rugby the All Blacks would ever play — an away game, a win.

One can only guess what Tom Ellison, who argued for player payment a hundred years earlier, would have made of it. Or Dave Gallaher, who represented an ideal of colonial manhood at a time before the sun set on the British Empire. Both were players in a greater game. Through rugby and war — often at the same time — New Zealanders began the search for identity, children of Empire, beginning to find their feet, still not quite sure where to call home. Some, like Gallaher, were born and died on foreign soil. Others, like Ellison, died where they were born. One at home and one away.

In your atlas two islands not in narrow seas
Like a child's kite anchored in the indifferent blue,
Two islands pointing from the Pole, upward
From the Ross Sea and the tall havenless ice:
Small trade and no triumph, men of strength
Proved at football and in wars not their own.

Allen Curnow
'Not in Narrow Seas', 1939

Part 2

GOLDEN YEARS

There's this huge generation gap, and yet, in many ways, there's no generation gap. Douglas was just telling us the other night about how he used to be a milk boy in Napier here. He used to get on his bike and he used to cycle out to the city limits. And he used to meet the horse-drawn cart and he used to fill up his dixies on the handlebars of his bike, and then he used to go around all the houses with his dipper and fill up their billy which was at the gate.

   And yet here's young Mac who demands fresh milk delivered to the door each day. It comes in plastic bottles or whatever. He expects to be able to order it in chocolate, raspberry or whatever flavour. So there's this huge generation difference. But they can still sit down on the couch, as they did the other night, and talk about rugby. And it's just man to man.

Bill Dalton

Three generations of Dalton men have grown up with rugby. Doug, the eldest, became an All Black in the 1930s. His son Bill played as a boy, gave it away in favour of motor racing, but never lost the love of watching the game. And Doug's grandson Mac now plays for his grandfather's old club, Napier Tech Old Boys. Doug was born the year before the outbreak of the First World War; Mac was born four decades after the end of the Second. The worlds they entered were completely different — Doug's being not all that removed from the nineteenth century, and Mac's a late twentieth century universe of home computers and video games. Yet rugby spans the decades, unchanged in its ability to draw people of all ages and backgrounds into deep discussion of the merits of this or that player, and the importance of an upcoming game. It has always been, in Bill Dalton's words, 'a great leveller'.

It was a point of conversational reference. I don't know whether it was all that deep. It was something a father could talk about to his youngest child and the youngest child could respond.

Ian Cross

Fathers and Sons

. . . rugby became a game again . . .

Trying to put an exact date on rugby's engagement of the popular imagination is futile. The game was long established as the national winter pastime by the First World War. But it had also been, in that first half-century, part of New Zealand's struggle for its own identity within the British Empire. By the 1920s, it can be argued, rugby had moved beyond being linked with various Victorian or Edwardian notions of manliness, muscular Christianity or imperial loyalty. After the dreadful effects of the war, rugby became a game again, and took on the dimensions that would make it the country's abiding obsession for the next half-century.

One needs to remember what appalling casualties New Zealand suffered fighting for the Empire. Of the slightly more than 100,000 New Zealanders who served overseas, well over half were killed or injured. In a tiny population, fifteen out of every thousand people were killed; not a soul was unaffected, not a town left without fewer young men. Pre-war jingoism became somewhat muted during the campaigns of Gallipoli and later the Western Front, and, while New Zealand's nationalism retained an imperial gloss, the country emerged from the war with a greater sense of itself. The self-image still tended to play up the frontier myths, when the country was, in fact, becoming a small-town society. But after the hell of war-torn Europe, it was a tranquil land. Returning troops reinforced the idea that New Zealand was God's own country, an ideal society. At the same time, it rapidly became a wowser nation, enforcing six o'clock closing for pubs, and developing a xenophobic distrust of foreigners and layabouts. The male institutions founded during the settler period — the pub and the football

Napier's McLean Park during the first golden era of Hawke's Bay rugby.
Bruce Hawkins Collection

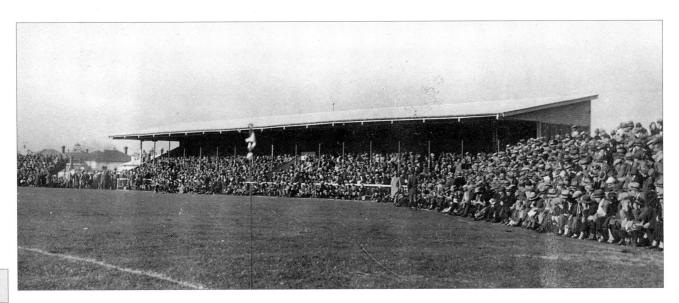

ground in particular — became very exclusive. Society was, in the words of Jock Phillips, 'highly gender segregated'. Men had work, the pub after work, and rugby on Saturday.

The mateship rituals nurtured by work and war found new outlets. There was a sense of putting war and its attendant horrors behind. Like other countries within the Empire, New Zealand went sport mad in the 1920s, with the biggest crowds for club games recorded in that decade (as in Britain, where soccer really flourished after the war).

> I think that within the confines of the rugby field, as behind the frosted windows of the pub, male culture was allowed to flower. I don't think men were ever arrested for swearing within a rugby ground. That was something one joked about and accepted. It was part of male culture. If one swore in public outside the rugby ground, and particularly if women were present, that was not acceptable.
>
> *Jock Phillips*

> It was a society very much determined to try and squeeze every ounce of enjoyment out of the years following the war. And that general sense of wanting to get on with things. I think all of it is grounded in this sense that life is there to be lived, and whatever your sporting preoccupation happens to be in the 20s, then you go for it. It's something to enjoy.
>
> *Len Richardson*

In Hawke's Bay, the young Doug Dalton was growing up in that climate of post-war promise. The region was modernising — it had electricity, trams, milking machines on the farms and a new rugby stadium. It also had the finest provincial rugby team in the country; among the stars at various times were George Nepia, Bert Cooke and the great Brownlie brothers, Cyril, Maurice and Laurence.

The thirteenth child of a working class Napier family, Doug loved rugby from the start — remarkable, really, considering his father, a cabby, scorned the game and described it as nothing better than 'brute force and ignorance'. One of his hobbies as a boy was to collect the front panels of Castle cigarette packets, which carried pictures of famous rugby players. Once you had collected enough, you could choose a poster-size version of the player of your choice. Douglas chose Maurice Brownlie — peerless loose forward and All Black for most of the period 1922 to 1928 — and hung the poster at the foot of his bed. 'That was what I strove for,' Doug remembered in his 80s. 'To be an All Black like Maurice Brownlie.'

Maurice Brownlie, hero of Hawke's Bay and All Black rugby, and idol of the young Douglas Dalton, future All Black forward himself.
Alexander Turnbull Library

41

What a team! The champion Hawke's Bay lineup of 1926, including George Nepia, Maurice Brownlie, Bert Cooke and Jimmy Mill.
Ross McKelvie

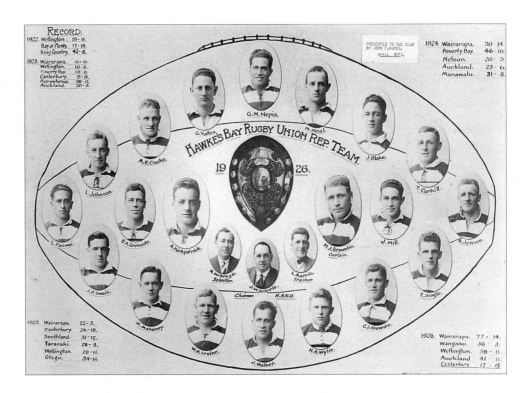

On Saturdays, Doug sold programmes at Napier's McLean Park. The crowds were consistently huge and wildly enthusiastic about the home team. This was the first great era of Hawke's Bay rugby, when they held the Ranfurly Shield from 1922 to 1927, defeating 24 challengers in all. The Hawke's Bay team played a generous, entertaining style of football by the standards of the day, helping establish the Shield as one of the world's great national rugby competitions.

. . . a generous, entertaining style of football by the standards of the day . . .

There was a different scrum in those days, a two-three-two formation with a wing forward. And the wing forward was a confounded nuisance to the opposing backs. The scrum, though, was very efficient. The ball came out so quickly that the half-back couldn't put it in. The wing forward put it in. So it did give a very quick heel, which meant that the backs could be got moving very quickly. From what I remember — not that I saw much; I was fairly young in the 1920s — but I did see a few games, and they did play an entertaining, running type of game.

rugby historian Neville McMillan

This was just 20 years after the Earl of Ranfurly, Governor of New Zealand, donated the 'log of wood' for the championship. Originally intended to be a cup, the shield that eventually arrived from England had been designed for a soccer competition, and had to be altered to suit the kind of football the colony preferred. Until the 1920s, the Shield had been held for many years by Auckland,

and briefly in Wellington and Taranaki, but had yet to become an institution. When Hawke's Bay took it off Wellington in 1922, Shield fever really started. The local newspapers carried extensive coverage of all the matches. People followed the team's fortunes religiously, and its amazing success encouraged enormous regional pride.

> Hawke's Bay had probably one of its greatest-ever teams. George Nepia was among them, and Bert Cooke. It began the whole ethos and fervour that is now associated with the Ranfurly Shield.
>
> *Ron Palenski*

> They had an excellent team. There were no weaknesses. They were nearly all All Blacks – no, there were actually All Blacks in the reserves at one stage! They played a winning brand of football which was very hard to combat. It certainly put Hawke's Bay on the map. Hawke's Bay was the rugby province for those years.
>
> *Neville McMillan*

> If the games had been played on Sunday there wouldn't have been any congregation whatsoever. Because the whole of the community was totally involved in this team.
>
> *T P McLean*

Rugby was becoming, as Jock Phillips discovered, a virtually perfect cross-section of the male population. His statistical analysis of All Blacks showed that their occupational and class profiles exactly matched the proportions in wider society. Even the stereotypes were accurate; backs being on average slightly better educated and professionally oriented than forwards.

> It was a game which spanned urban professionals right through to farmers and the working class, urban and rural people. I guess that is one of the most remarkable things about rugby. It was particularly in the 1920s, I think, that it became a universal experience for nearly all New Zealand men.
>
> *Jock Phillips*

A STAR IS BORN

New Zealanders found in their rugby heroes a universal expression of their own values. In the early 1920s, from out of nowhere, the country's latest (and perhaps greatest) sporting superstar emerged. George Nepia was a glamorous player for a glamorous age. Very handsome and preternaturally talented with a football, he

. . . it became a universal experience for nearly all New Zealand men.

43

George Nepia shows them how it's done at Rangitukia, near the East Cape, about 1955.
Alexander Turnbull Library

went from the back of beyond in a country at the bottom of the world, to fame on an international stage. In George Nepia, rugby found one of its best exemplars; the gentleman with the devastating tackle, the hard man with matinee idol looks, the Maori genius of an English game. He even wrote, with T P McLean, one of the best rugby books of all time, *I, George Nepia*. McLean explains the legend in his introduction:

> Within a few months, the boy who had been a hero to only to a few bare-footed kids playing around the fringes of the field had become a hero in every strata of society, from royalty down. His name had become, as it has remained, a household word. He was a legend, mystic, wonderful . . . Truly, George Nepia was more than a Golden Boy of the Golden Years of Rugby. He was the man who became, rightly or wrongly, the personification of his period.
>
> I have this crazy view of George Nepia. I think he's the nation's first genuine sporting hero. It seems to me he was a hero waiting to happen. He just plays so beautifully, so courageously, that in many ways I think he captures the spirit of the age. A really, truly great rugby player.
>
> *Len Richardson*

44

Nepia leapt to prominence as the indefatigable fullback of the 1924 'Invincible' All Blacks on their tour of Great Britain and France; the 'last line of defence' who played in every game of the tour, 30 matches, at a rate of two a week, for four months. He was still a teenager and new to the No. 15 position. On a previous tour of Australia he'd played badly. Not a lot was known about him, not a lot was expected. But Nepia emerged from the tour an immortal.

Born in 1905 at Wairoa, he grew up the hard way; raised by his widowed grandmother but with a domineering father always in the background. In his autobiography he recalls being a timid player to begin with. 'My father was ashamed of me and disgusted with me. He once came on to the field while I was playing and clouted me on the backside as hard as he could; it did no good that I was aware of.' At the height of his career, however, Nepia was renowned for his fearless play, and his son Oma remembers George saying that rugby injuries 'are like medals; you wear them with pride'.

Like so many great Maori players before him, George was to be educated at Te Aute College. But he never made it to that citadel of Maori rugby, leaving the train early at Hastings and enrolling at the Maori Agricultural College instead. This was a Mormon school, and young George learnt from the elders the arts of punting and crash tackling. Along with his cousin, Lui Paewai (also to become an Invincible), George was spotted by the doyen of Hawke's Bay rugby, Norman McKenzie, and selected to play for Napier. From that point on it was a proverbial meteoric rise to stardom, first with Hawke's Bay and then the All Blacks. In all, Nepia played only nine tests for New Zealand, but his reputation outshines those of players with very many more caps.

> Well, he was one of these fellows who created an awe about himself. It was not that he was in any way a guy who bragged about himself. He let his own experiences on the paddock speak for themselves. I think the fact that he mastered the skills of this game, and was able to exhibit it in what was then considered to be the home of rugby, in England, and do it better than anybody else at that time — that captured the imagination of all the people of the British Isles, and the press.
>
> *Jim Perry*

Despite being fêted abroad, meeting royalty and getting more than a glimpse of how the other half lived, Nepia remained the East Coast farmer that he'd always been. Having married his Ngati Porou wife, Huinga, he moved to Rangitukia near the East Cape, and ran dairy cows on a small block near the

Nepia was renowned for his fearless play . . .

45

local rugby ground. His daughter Kiwi Rowlands, who still lives in the old family home, describes George as the quintessential country gentleman, albeit not a wealthy one. Milking was man's work, and no ladies were allowed to lend a hand. Kiwi and her mother would take him tea and cake — he had a very sweet tooth — while he worked on the farm. He had a fine singing voice, as can be heard in recordings of his tender rendition of 'Neath the Maori Moon', and the family often sang together. His own painful experiences of childhood, she says, made him a determinedly good and even-tempered father. And he was terribly protective of his daughter; woe betide any suitor who didn't follow his every instruction to the letter.

Jim Perry arrived in the Nepia household as a boy, having been removed from the relatives who were raising him badly, and removed again from the care of foster parents who had used him as little more than a slave milker (he remembers milking 74 cows alone at the age of nine). He was driven up the East Coast by a welfare officer who took his own father, an Englishman, along for the ride to

Nepia leads the 1924 All Blacks in the haka, Swansea, 1924.
NZ Rugby Museum

meet the great George Nepia. When Perry failed to recognise the name, the Englishman told him, 'There's something wrong with you boy.' But Jim simply hadn't heard of Nepia. 'As far as I was concerned he was just another farmer who wanted someone to milk his cows.' It was only later, by reading his foster father's meticulously kept scrapbooks from the 1924 tour, that he learned the truth for himself.

George was a kinder man than his previous guardians, and only ever raised a hand to Jim once — 'and I deserved it'. He remembers the man, not the myth; a sprightly figure with an impish sense of humour (George, in later life, would occasionally trick gullible reporters into believing he was only 16 when he toured Great Britain). In the tiered rural society of the East Coast, George was one of the few Maori men to move with equal ease among Pakeha and Maori — not just because of his rugby reputation, but because of his naturally dignified demeanour. He remained modest. According to Kiwi, when George visited South Africa as a guest of the South African Rugby Union in 1976, he was treated like royalty and even offered a new Mercedes to take home with him; he declined.

> When I met him I didn't see him as a famous person. He was just another Maori milking cows and trying to make a living. But I got to know him very well. He was an even-tempered bloke. I only ever saw him get really angry once, in the whole time that I was living with him, right up until the time he died. I guess that was part of the thing about him as a rugby player — that he could keep his cool all the way through a game. Just as he did when everyday things affected him.
>
> *Jim Perry*

The 1924 All Blacks consolidated the reputation of New Zealand rugby established by the 1905 Originals, and avenged the one loss of that earlier team with a mighty 19-0 thrashing of Wales. As had been the case in 1905, politicians took a keen interest in the national team, with the Prime Minister William Massey and his deputy Gordon Coates even moved to gently lobby for selection changes after early criticism of player standards. After the triumphant tour, of course, they were falling over themselves to congratulate the Invincible heroes. Former government minister and High Commissioner in London, William Pember Reeves, was moved to eulogise the now-famous fullback:

> Kia toa! New Zealand! See
> Nepia guards the gate.

. . . he was treated like royalty . . .

All vantage points were taken when the All Blacks avenged the 1905 loss to Wales in 1924.
NZ Rugby Museum

47

A rock and a house of defence is he,
A tino tangata great.

In the days of strict amateurism, of course, such tributes were never transformed into cash. Life on a small East Coast farm was hard for anyone, All Blacks no exception. New Zealand's sputtering post-war economy often meant a life of near-subsistence farming for Maori families in the remotest parts of the country. As the decade drew to an end, George Nepia, like everyone else, would feel the full effects of the Great Depression.

THE FAME GAME

Amateurism had been enshrined as a fundamental tenet of rugby after the First World War. While New Zealand would engage in regular debates within the English-dominated International Rugby Union over various laws of the game, it would be a long time before this particular dogma was seriously challenged. At the same time, as the country's dominant sport, rugby was making men famous. Well before the advent of sponsorship and product endorsement, All Blacks were trading on their names in a way that could never be called professionalism, but which ineluctably linked their livelihoods with their rugby careers. An All Black reputation was a business asset — never more so than in the retail menswear sector. The great names of Bob Scott, Charlie Saxton, Ponty Reid, Tom Morrison and Andy Leslie were all at one time or another on shop windows as well as rugby programmes.

The first great player to exploit his name in this way was Nepia's fellow Invincible, Bert Cooke. Another rugby genius, Bert was a small man with a huge heart (he apparently convinced the tour brochure publishers to add a stone to his weight, thereby exaggerating his tiny eight-and-a-half-stone frame). Many still rate him as highly or higher than Nepia as an instinctive player of the game, a devastatingly effective running back with the biggest try tally of the 1924 team. He was described in the tour booklet as, 'elusive as a shadow; strikes like lightning, flashes with brilliancy, Cooke is the shining star of the side. He is meteoric in method; penetrates like a bayonet-point, and thrusts like steel. Cooke is Eclipse!' Not your average menswear salesman, in other words.

Cooke's first-class record gives some indication of his peripatetic lifestyle; at some stage in his career he played for Auckland, Hawke's Bay, Wairarapa and Wellington. He had already learned the menswear trade working at Smith and

Bert had one great failing as a businessman — he had no brains whatever for the job.

Caughey in Auckland, which kept him on half-wages during the British tour. Later he moved to Hawke's Bay where he starred in the Ranfurly Shield and provincial competitions, especially the team's great 1926 season. According to T P McLean, Norman McKenzie engineered a job for Cooke at Jack Snaddon's Napier menswear outlet. There were misgivings about Bert's ability to manage his own finances, something to which McKenzie was privy as an officer of the Post Office Savings Bank. But Cooke avoided any difficulty when, the following year, he was effectively poached by Wairarapa, where £600 was put up to establish him as a partner in Hendry and Cooke Menswear. Masterton was a prosperous town, with a large freezing works and several hosiery mills, but it was hard hit by the Depression. Cooke is said to have fallen out with Hendry due to his tendency to donate rather than sell to worthy cases.

The 'shining star of the side', 1924 Invincible Bert Cooke.
NZ Rugby Museum

> Bert had one great failing as a businessman — he had no brains whatever for the job. [Norman] McKenzie told me that a mother would come in, in those harsh winters you can get in Masterton, with a son this high in ragged clothes. The boy would walk out with a full set of clothes and the mother would say, 'How much, Mr Cooke?' And he'd say, 'On me, lady, on me.'
>
> *T P McLean*

> My father-in-law lived in Masterton at the time that Cooke was playing there, and he has told me that Cooke's business failed because he spent too much time yakking about football to the customers, and he was apparently trading his mates at mates' rates fairly well.
>
> *Neville McMillan*

Cooke was instrumental in Wairarapa taking the Shield off Hawke's Bay, and performed a legendary tackle on his former team-mate, the fourteen-stone Maurice Brownlie. After three years in Masterton, he moved on again, this time to Wellington where the Union sponsored him into his own store in Lower Hutt. Once more, he was the key to his adopted home's rugby fortunes, helping Wellington take the Shield from Southland. None of his ventures in menswear was particularly successful, nor was his last attempt in the late 1930s. But it seems clear that he did draw patrons to the shops, and others were as content to profit from the Cooke name as Bert was. Much as the English might have hated it, there was an innate tension within an amateur sport that turned players into national or international figures.

BELEAGUERED

Cooke had returned from the 1924 tour a folk hero. He was a garrulous, fun-loving man who loved the company of other men. 'It didn't matter where you went,' says his son Maurice, 'people were always singing out to him and coming over to shake his hand.' He liked a drink too, and found a ready welcome in bars. 'He'd walk in and sure enough there'd be a few beers sent over for him,' Maurice recalls. 'I used to try and help him drink them if I could.'

Like George Nepia, Bert Cooke's life was determined by his ability to earn a crust. All Black icon or no, they were working-class men in an era of great economic instability. When the Depression struck with full force it had as much impact on New Zealanders' way of thinking as it did on their hip pockets or their larders. This was an international crisis of capital, not some localised slump that would pass. Not only was the old colonial economy rocked off its hinges, but

A soup kitchen in Wellington during the Depression of the 1930s. Rugby was often the only relief from the tedium and insecurity of joblessness.
Evening Post Collection, Alexander Turnbull Library

colonial ideas about thrift and virtue were revealed as simplistic and even stupid. Government strategies of wage cuts, retrenched social spending and semi-penal work camps drove many among the disaffected lower classes to seek refuge in the socialist alternatives offered by the Labour Party, which doubled its vote in the decade after 1928.

Down on the farm in Rangitukia, George Nepia and his family struggled through the Depression as best they could. Through the late 20s and early 30s the land yielded a 'dismally low income', as he described it in *I, George Nepia*. 'A young family occupied that farm, all in need of the clothing, the care, the attention for which money must be earned . . . It was a grey world. There seemed not much prospect of improvement. Only a year or so before, thousands had rioted through the streets of New Zealand's main cities in the demand for work and food and social justice. No one who ever lived through that Depression as an adult or adolescent could ever forget the cruel experience.'

Nepia tells us this in the context of his hardship's most direct personal consequence; his switch to rugby league for the London club of Streatham and Mitcham in 1935. He was paid £500 to go — not willingly, but with some relief that debts could be paid and plans made for his children's welfare. 'I say, too, that if the Labour Government had come into power with the guaranteed price scheme for butterfat in 1934 instead of 1935, I would not have gone.'

Three years earlier, Bert Cooke had encountered the same thing. After leaving Wellington, he had returned to Hawke's Bay to help repair his father-in-law's orchard in Hastings after the devastating earthquake of 1931. But a season of rugby was all he could afford before chasing work north to Auckland, finally finding employment in a butter factory near Te Aroha. He accepted an offer to play league for the Richmond club that included a job in Auckland. 'In those days money meant a lot,' says Maurice Cooke, 'so we came to Auckland and he played for Richmond.' Cooke adapted to the new code well, representing Auckland and captaining the Kiwis for three tests. Older rugby fans might have grumbled, 'but by the same token they could see that things were tough, and he had a wife and kids to look after, so he took the option to put us first, I think'.

> I can remember him playing league against the English team in 1932, and they had a huge wing who weighed over fourteen stone. As he was coming down the side line, Cooke went across and hit him and he went down like a sack of spuds. He didn't care how big they were, he'd tackle anything.
>
> *Neville McMillan*

. . . and he went down like a sack of spuds.

HARD TIMES

A lot changed and a lot stopped during the Depression — but not rugby. In a way, the game was forced back to its roots as an ideal sport for an unbroken land. Some bare ground and a pig's bladder was all one needed, and rugby in New Zealand had retained its rough-and-ready nature. Players made do with balls that had long since lost their shape. Kids played barefoot. One of them, Bob Scott, would one day make kicking in bare feet something of a trade mark.

Scott's family was torn apart by the Depression. His mother left while they lived in the tiny Taranaki town of Tangarakau, and all the children spent some time in orphanages. Later, while his brothers and sister were put in a home in Auckland, Bob and his father (who had been badly wounded in the First World War) moved from rooming house to rooming house. There was really only one other form of escapism in those days — films — but even this was out of reach for many. That left rugby.

Repairing second-hand boots in 1932 — for those who could afford them.
Alexander Turnbull Library

We always played in bare feet in those days. Right through the schooldays, right up until I was about fifteen years of age. It wasn't really until I was getting on for fifteen that I wore shoes anyhow . . . I could always kick in bare feet because of those days back in the Depression when you didn't wear boots.

I think it was about the only outlet they had, other than going to the pictures. Because a lot of those other sports were fairly minor in those days. Even cricket didn't have the strength it has today. Rugby was virtually the ultimate. I mean, it was the only outlet they had as far as recreation was concerned.

Bob Scott, All Black 1946–54

I think rugby was a panacea. The blokes turned out, they hadn't got a cracker, but they used to play their club games with vigour. Few of them had money . . . During those difficult years, rugby was a kinship. Rugby was, as I say, the opium of the Kiwi people at that stage.

T P McLean

Obviously as the Depression hit there was increasing concern about men's role as providers, and a great deal of anxiety and concern that some men were unable to provide for themselves. And it's said that during the Depression rugby particularly flowered because it provided a kind of compensation for men who were either unemployed or didn't find a way of expressing their manhood through their jobs.

Jock Phillips

For Doug Dalton, by this time working as a plasterer's apprentice in Napier, the equation was simple. 'Rugby was the only game you could afford to play.' While Bert Cooke was repairing his father-in-law's orchard in Hastings, Dalton was helping to rebuild Napier. The 1931 quake had struck while he and a partner were working in a room at the Napier Girls High School. Unfamiliar with the building, they had tried to run out the long way. Dalton made it, but his mate was trapped by a collapsing brick wall and later died of his injuries. Coming on top of the economic disaster of the Depression, this natural disaster did at least create work for the legions of unemployed.

On the day of a big concrete pour the foreman would go out and pick out half a dozen men, put them behind the mixer, and there would be thirty or forty men lined on the footpath waiting for a job. Some chaps had never done any manual work in their lives. Some of them couldn't even go home at night. They'd go to sleep on the cement . . . My being an apprentice boy and a plasterer, thank goodness I missed all that. But it was tough with plasterers too. They were getting a shilling an hour and a share of the profits from the sub-contractors. And of course there was never any share of the profits. That was it. A shilling an hour.

Doug Dalton

Doug Dalton finally realised his dream to be an All Black forward like Maurice Brownlie in 1935, when he was selected for the tour of Great Britain and Ireland. Things hadn't changed much since the Invincibles set sail ten years earlier, or even the Originals twenty years before. The team was forbidden from playing in the six weeks prior to embarking for the ship journey (to avoid injuries), which, combined with a month-long sea voyage, took its toll on fitness. They weighed themselves on a hook in the butcher's shop in the bowels of the ship, and practised with a scrum machine on the deck. There were a total of four supporters with the team — a wealthy Wellington businessman and his wife, and two fans from Westport. Like their predecessors, the 1935 All Blacks received three shillings a day in the form of a chit to be spent only in the hotel. Players had already had to come up with £30 of their own before being allowed on the tour. On his return in 1936, Dalton was re-employed by his old boss (who had been paying

Rugby was, as I say, the opium of the Kiwi people at that stage.

Prime Minister Michael Joseph Savage further endears himself to the population, 1940.
Alexander Turnbull Library

. . . it reinforced a belief that 'individual skill and character mattered'.

him 25 shillings a week during the tour as well), rejoined the rugby club and tried to patch up a courtship interrupted by rugby.

But this resumption of normal life belied a profound political change in New Zealand. Five years of serious Depression had destroyed the various remnants of old parties that had become the Coalition Government. Michael Joseph Savage's Labour Party, offering the only alternative to the incumbent's failure to cure the country's economic paralysis, extended its support from the towns and cities into the rural electorates. The urban poor and the small farmer had, in effect, created a new consensus that would see state power greatly increased, welfare payments restored, guaranteed prices for primary products introduced and an insulated local market created with import and export controls. The last was, incidentally, a great boon for rugby outfitters, especially bootmakers. Up until 1938, locally made boots competed with Australian and British imports. But from that time on, companies like Ideal Shoes of Wellington (which shod the 1924 Invincibles with boots containing gramophone springs in the sole to give them flexibility), had the market to themselves — until another Labour government opened the market to foreign brands in the 1980s.

In the process of giving everyone a fair go, writes historian Eric Olssen, Labour also began the rapid modernisation of the state. The bureaucracy expanded, and a technocratic class began to operate the machinery of government. New Zealanders, Olssen suggests, took solace in their sport, in particular rugby, at a time when industrial society seemed increasingly impersonal and mechanistic. Rugby not only reinforced the pioneer myth, it reinforced a belief that 'individual skill and character mattered'. While much in life could seem to be beyond people's control, 'rugby reassured New Zealanders that man, if not woman, was still the master of his fate, the captain of his soul'.

BEHIND EVERY GREAT PLAYER ...

It has always been faintly ludicrous to speak of rugby as the expression of national character, or the repository of collective dreams, when it is only played by half the population (modern women's rugby notwithstanding). The national game is often held as evidence that New Zealand is 'a man's country', by definition brutal, insensitive and probably misogynistic. But without denying the large influence of a culture created from the preoccupations of single men and wild colonial boys, there's an obvious corollary: boys have mothers, men have wives and women have sons and husbands. It seems too easy to consign 'the fairer sex' to some invisible sock-washing role in the background, while the other lot got on with forging something called national identity.

Undeniably there was a division of labour – the men worked for victory on the paddock and the ladies worked to keep them going. But the rugby club was also one of the few social centres between the wars. Communities grew around it, love affairs blossomed at Saturday night dances, and friends stayed in touch through the comfortable routines of rugby. In the Auckland suburb of Onehunga, at the local Manukau Rovers rugby club, Florence Leng carved out a life as rich and rewarding as any man in a muddy jersey. Her father was vice-president of the club and her brother played. Every Saturday in winter she watched the footy, and watched the coaches' wives organise everything behind the scenes. Next door lived Mick Williams, club secretary (and one-time president of the Auckland Union), and his wife, Fairy. It wasn't her real name, but she worked such miracles for the players that one of them gave her the nickname and everyone knew her as Fairy until she died. She was a second mother to many of the

. . . the rugby club was also one of the few social centres between the wars.

The once-familiar sight of football jerseys hung out to dry, the ensigns of women's role in a male drama. Wellington, 1930s.
W Hall Raine Collection, Alexander Turnbull Library

players, giving them shelter if they had too far to go home on Saturday nights, feeding them and washing their clothes — spreading the mud-caked jerseys on the lawn in the hope it would rain.

Well, it was a whole week's job getting the jerseys and things done, because there were no washing machines or anything like that. No dryers, no nothing! And quite often on Saturday morning she'd have the fire going. She had a coal range and she had the jerseys on top, on the tray to air them off. It was hard work and they were not jerseys as they are today. They were great hefty things. I don't know, they said they were cotton, but there was more than cotton. I think there was lead in them too! When they were wet they were terrible.

Mrs Williams was a rugby widow, really. There was nothing else in her life but rugby. She lived for it herself. It was lucky that she was so interested in it. She even had a budgie barracking for Manukau all the time. It would go on and on until you'd have to tell it to shut up. It was just so bad! 'Pack around Manukau, hook that ball Manukau.' All that sort of thing.

The dances were the highlight of everything. All the boys used to come. It wasn't one team, it was the whole lot. A lot of Onehunga people now, they used to go to the dances when they were just young kids. They still talk about those dances . . . That was our life. Football, and then rush home and have tea and rush back again to the dances. That was our life.

Florence Leng

There was nothing else in her life but rugby.

WAR GAMES

Just 20 years after the war to end all wars, the sons of those who survived the first expedition were again sent off to fight. The dutiful Dominion stood fast by Britain's side. New Zealand's place in the affections of the British had been boosted in 1936, at the Berlin Olympic Games, when Jack Lovelock won the 1500 metres in front of Hitler and the Nazi élite. Britain won no medals that year, but her national anthem played in the stadium anyway. The Empire was very much alive, and New Zealanders remained the faithful, farthest-flung branch of the family. When war came in 1939, Michael Joseph Savage announced the country's allegiance to Britain: 'Where she goes, we go. Where she stands, we stand.'

Conscription was introduced later, but the first fighting force was easily formed from volunteers. As had occurred 25 years earlier, at the start of the First World War, sports clubs became a logical recruiting ground. College Rifles in Auckland, for example, had its own military tradition, having been formed in 1897 from a combination of schools and the Rifle Brigade. Army recruitment officers visited the club's training ground in April 1939, and twelve players signed up that night. Of the club's 90-odd players that year, 39 had been killed by the end of the war. New Zealand men enjoyed their male institutions, and the expression of mateship through rugby led naturally to its expression in war.

> I saw a lot of my old rugby players joining up, and I decided to go away with them. Being half Maori, I didn't have to go, but I felt it was my duty for our country that I join them.
>
> *H W 'Mick' Kenny*

> People think of war as battles, but actually most of what war is about is sitting around doing nothing. How do you occupy people for that long period of time, sitting around waiting? One way is march on the parade ground, but that's not a very engaged experience. Another way is to play rugby, because at least people put passion and intensity into it. They strengthen themselves physically, they learn to work together as a team, they think about strategy and tactics. So to that extent it's a perfect accompaniment to war training, and it was very much used like that right through the Second World War.
>
> *Jock Phillips*

New Zealand soldiers in North Africa during World War II — perfect training for battle, and a break from the monotony of war.
War History Collection, Alexander Turnbull Library

No, not surrender. New Zealand cavalry officers and NCOs teaching Syrian mountain villagers the finer points of the lineout, May 1942.
War History Collection, Alexander Turnbull Library

Rugby was played constantly during the war, both at home and abroad, by services teams. Anywhere that a sizeable group of New Zealanders congregated — including prisoner-of-war camps — a game (or at least a kick-around) was usually got together. Even on the inhospitable tropical islands of the Pacific, rugby games took place (Doug Dalton remembers clearing rocks from a field before playing an exhibition match for US servicemen in New Caledonia). In North Africa, the first competition between battalions and units was organised only weeks after the arrival of the Second Expeditionary Force in Egypt, and the standard of play so impressed the Divisional Commander, General Bernard Freyberg, that he presented a trophy — the Freyberg Cup — for future competitions.

Freyberg himself embodied a lot of New Zealand's recent history. English-born, but raised and educated in Wellington, he won the Victoria Cross on the Somme in 1916. When war broke out again, he was invited by the Savage government to command the New Zealand Division in the Middle East. He became Governor-General after the war, and was made a lord in 1951, spending the rest of his life as Deputy Constable and Lieutenant-Governor of Windsor Castle. Like New Zealand, he lived in two worlds, the old and the new. And he certainly understood New Zealanders, if his enthusiasm for the 'soldier-making game' was any guide.

9.

The intensity of old school rivalries plays on the faces of first fifteen members from St Patrick's College Silverstream, on the day of their big 1995 clash with brother school, St Patrick's College in Wellington. The fighting spirit of New Zealand rugby is kept alive in the hard fought battles of secondary schools competitions.

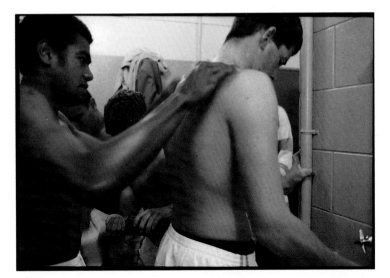

10.
The boys of St Pat's Silverstream have inherited a passionate rugby ethos established by the school's devout Irish founders. But as the century draws to an end, fewer and fewer New Zealand schools reflect the once-universal devotion to the game that peaked after World War II.

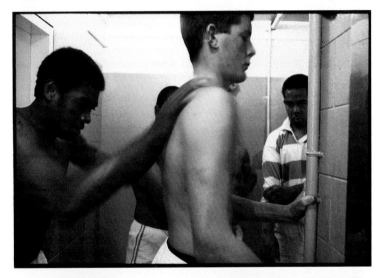

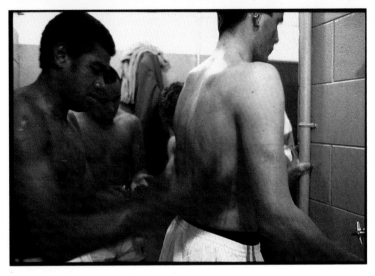

11.
Like a mini-national championship game, the St Pat's versus St Pat's battle comes complete with show business trappings. Perhaps only those who have been to an all-boys school can truly appreciate the way the rugby paddock becomes the fever pitch on a day like today.

12.
*Rugby, rosary and
Pacific Island culture;
the modern Catholic
school invents new
traditions to pick up
where the old ones left
off. St Patrick's
Silverstream,
Wellington, 1995*

When we were worrying about a game, or concentrating on it, we didn't have to worry about the rigours of war or anything like that. It was erased from our minds — worrying about going into action. Rugby satisfied us . . . if we went up by transport to the desert, we always had a rugby ball in the truck. And as soon as the truck stopped we'd be out kicking the ball around in our army gear, in our army boots.

H W 'Mick' Kenny

Kenny, who until he was injured, vied with Bob Scott as the Division's best fullback, took part in one of the most extraordinary rugby games ever played. Freyberg had challenged the South African commander to an impromptu international. This was soon after the disastrous New Zealand evacuation from Greece and Crete, and the General had to be persuaded by his aide-de-camp, Jack Griffiths (pre-war All Black and captain of the 19th Battalion team), to postpone the match until the troops had recuperated. The best players from various units were assembled to form a team, and a large stretch of hard sand at Sidi Haneish, near the New Zealand headquarters, was earmarked for a pitch. Colonel Alan Andrews, later to manage the 2NZEF 'Kiwis' rugby team, took appropriate precautions in case of enemy attack.

Jack Finlay of 25 New Zealand Battalion at the Division football competition, Castelraimondo, Italy, 1944. War History Collection, Alexander Turnbull Library

Two or three destroyers parked out in the sea nearby. I got the airforce to put a couple of squadrons of fighters out in a screen around the area. We had two regiments of ack-ack guns — ours and the South Africans' — posted in the sandhills adjacent to the ground. We couldn't do much more than that.

All the South African and the Kiwis came to view the match, and I made them park a mile or so away from the ground and walk in — march in — because I felt if any airforce did come over, they'd be more likely to attack a big conglomeration of vehicles, rather than men. I suppose it must have been ten thousand South Africans at least, and ten thousand New Zealanders, and they formed up around the ground and the great match took place.

And we had a great victory! A narrow victory, but it was a victory and that was the main thing. And that's the only time the New Zealand Division played as a divisional team throughout the whole war.

Alan Andrews

Several thousand soldiers gathered to watch the game . . .

It was not, however, the only time that New Zealanders played South Africans in the desert. Immediately before the battle of El Alamein a game was staged behind the allied lines on the orders of Field Marshal Montgomery, who thought that enemy reconnaissance aircraft would surely conclude that no major offensive was planned if games of football were taking place. One of the players in that match, Louis Babrow, a pre-war Springbok, recounted the events for Radio New Zealand in the 1960s. Several thousand soldiers gathered to watch the game, which the New Zealanders won, he related. There was some suggestion that German aircraft did spot the game, and that intelligence reports suggested allied morale was so low that they had begun fighting among themselves. Of the 30 players in the decoy game, half were killed, wounded or taken prisoner in the decisive battle which began two nights later.

> New Zealanders are pretty aggressive people . . . to a degree they were a law unto themselves and yet a great team people. I think it was a fact that the way they played their rugby was the way they were involved in the war.
>
> *Bob Scott*

The theory that New Zealanders fought as they played — hard, and to win — was by now an accepted truth. Since the Boer War, when the volunteers from 'Maoriland' had seemed so physically imposing to the British, New Zealanders had come to view themselves as 'territorials of Empire', as Jock Phillips expresses it. The writer John Mulgan took the notion further in his *Report on Experience*, published in 1947, two years after his death (apparently by suicide) in Cairo. 'I found in war-time that there was a considerable virtue in men who had played games like professionals to win, and not, like public-school boys and amateurs, for exercise,' he wrote. The passage from which these words come is one of the favourite quotations of rugby fans looking for a literary clue to the seductive power of the national game. 'Rugby football was the best of all our pleasures: it was religion and desire and fulfilment all in one,' wrote Mulgan, having already observed that, 'We were a naive society and I suppose a little crude . . . Our main pursuits were only cultural in the broadest sense.'

What is often missing from the rose-tinted recitation of Mulgan's words is their broader context. He believed passionately in the rightness of the war, and was attempting to find an explanation for his countrymen's emotional adaptability to battle. Those who believed that an 'exaggerated attention to games gives the young a wrong sense of values' may be right, he argued. But he could live with that when it came to fighting for your life. 'So that perhaps it would be more correct to say that the virtues and values of the New Zealanders were not so much wrong as primitive, and to this extent useful in the current collapse of civilisation.'

When Mulgan declared that 'New Zealanders, when they went to war, found

Rugby football was the best of all our pleasures . . .

it easier to get down to the moral plane of a German soldier,' he actually meant it as a compliment. He didn't think such an ability precluded ordinary human decency outside wartime, or that it detracted from the 'natural kindliness' of Kiwis. 'It was only that they looked on war as a game, and a game to New Zealanders is something that they play to win, against the referee, if necessary. Personally, I still prefer games that way and find them more interesting.'

> There was an American writer who wrote a PhD thesis called 'These New Zealanders', and he posed the question: what is it that makes the New Zealander the best light infantry soldier in the world? And he went on to examine various reasons, and one of them he pulled out was our love for rugby football . . . He believed that the aggression that we showed on the rugby field — no mates, no prisoners taken — carried over into our fighting. He could have something there.
>
> *Neville McMillan*

At war's end a New Zealand Army team, to be known simply as the 'Kiwis', was selected from troops in Egypt and Europe for a tour of Britain, France and

Germany. They played from late 1945 to the end of March, 1946, won 29 games, lost two and drew two. Of the 29-strong squad, 16 would go on to become All Blacks after the war. Captain Charlie Saxton had already been an All Black in 1938. On Freyberg's instructions, the team suppressed the instincts that John Mulgan so eloquently described, and played to entertain.

We had to play the way he wanted us to play — open rugby football.

Freyberg was very keen that we should do particularly well, but was adamant that we weren't to go out there to win at all costs. We had to play the way he wanted us to play — open rugby football. As time went on, he became more and more pleased with the effort of the team, because they were winning and at the same time were playing the type of football he wanted us to play.

Alan Andrews

On their return to New Zealand the Kiwis kept on playing, dog-tired from years of war and still not properly reunited with loved ones. They took on five provincial sides, displaying their customary flair, thrilling crowds hungry for first-class football. In the first game, Auckland entered into the spirit and the two teams played to a scintillating 20-all draw. By the final match against Wellington, however, the exhausted Kiwis finally succumbed to a team that played to win, not merely to entertain. It was to set the tone for years to come (some would say until Charlie Saxton and Fred Allen revived open rugby after 1966).

As so often happens, other teams get the idea – we can combat this, tighten it up, neglect your outside backs, play ten man rugby. And that pattern did tend to follow in the late 40s. Ten man rugby was the in thing. It was winning rugby. It was dreadful stuff to look at!

Neville McMillan

AFTERMATH AND AFTERMATCH

The years immediately following the war found New Zealand, like every allied nation, revelling in peace and the promise of a hard-won better world. Depression and conflict coming on top of each other had created a strong collective appetite for security and stability. Jobs, homes and family life were the things New Zealanders craved. Couples married very young and went to bed early to create a baby boom. The national passion for rugby would become one of the cornerstones of the new contentment.

The country inevitably broadened its horizons, with so many returned soldiers having seen a wide, exotic world, and got its first literary journal in 1947 when *Landfall* was published. But football remained the people's poetry. The cold war had begun, and New Zealand began to shift its loyalties from Britain to another imperial superpower, America. In rugby, of course, New Zealand was a superpower itself. The game provided an alternative history for a nation weary (or wary) of conventional geopolitics. As the main character observes in Greg McGee's play, *Foreskin's Lament*, 'We who know our history by itineraries — the cold war of the 50s you say? Oh yes, we remember it well, those front-row problems, Skinner and Bekker.' McGee set the play in 1976, the year of the infamous All Black tour of South Africa that caused the African boycott of the Montreal Olympics. But as its title says, it is a lament for an era now passed, the post-war era when rugby truly did capture the spirit of an age. Tupper, the 'rip-shit-and-bust' coach, is that era made flesh. In the cruel words of another character, however, he is a 'dying breed', 'just an old fart left over from the Second World War'. As Michael Neill wrote in a forward to the play, 'When myths no longer serve to incarnate the values of a people, the customs that declare its sense of family, they become the maudlin properties of a lying nostalgia.'

Of course, in the late 1940s and 50s, Tupper was a young man. In war and rugby he would have found similar virtues; what one writer, quoted in Michael King's *New Zealanders At War*, described as 'the undoubted charms of soldiering . . . the drill, the high standard of discipline, the absence of worry about food, shelter, lodging, health'. Just about everything the rugby club provides, in other words. Like the surviving men of College Rifles, who revived the club over a few beers after the war, New Zealand men found both continuity and solace in the comradeship of rugby. The game lay at the centre of national life, and at the centre of domestic routine.

> Our house actually revolved around rugby. There were always rugby people at the house. My mother was always cooking extra meals because guys were in the house and people were coming to stay. On Saturday we used to have the option of going to the rugby with Douglas or going to the matinee movies. I must say, very often I chose the matinee, but in later years, of course, I thoroughly enjoyed

. . . rugby truly did capture the spirit of an age.

Rugby on the radio and milk in the cows; the steady rhythms of life after the war.
National Publicity Studios Collection, Alexander Turnbull Library

63

going to the rugby with Douglas. I would never have gone to a movie when there was a game of rugby to see, especially if I got the chance of going with Douglas.

Bill Dalton

Rugby, says Thelma, has kept them together.

Rugby provided the continuity in people's lives. When Thelma McSweeney married her husband Pete, she entered a close-knit circle of friends who had known each other since attending the Marist Brothers school in Auckland's Ponsonby. They were the children of working families from all parts of the city. Catholicism brought them together. Rugby, says Thelma, has kept them together. On leaving school, they played for the Marist club — just some of the countless New Zealanders who learned their rugby with their rosary. Nearly 50 years on, they can all remember the words to the Marist football song, and the circle remains unbroken.

Rugby came to dominate the McSweeney household, from the moment they cut short their honeymoon so that Pete could get back in time for a particularly important club match. Later, Pete had his teeth knocked out in a game. It didn't worry him, says Thelma, 'It was all part of the game, part of being a man and growing up.' When he lost his false teeth during a match, she remembers, both teams scoured the field afterwards until they were found. The men took over a back room in the old Aurora tavern, using it as a clubroom after training and on Saturday nights. They dubbed it the Vatican, and it became one of the centres of a rich social life based around rugby. When Pete died, it was his rugby comrades and their wives who rallied around.

The wives in particular have been fantastic. If you had bad times, they were there. They were there for the good times and the bad times, and we're all the same with each other. If there's anything sad in anyone's life, we're all there for each other.

Thelma McSweeney

To the dismay of a lot of men, some women showed a keen interest in actually playing rugby, not merely washing up after it. The games they managed to organise were often treated as novelties, but also displayed quite a radical break with their traditional roles. Once, it would have been like breaking a taboo. When games were being touted as the right tonic for racial fitness and imperial fortitude at the turn of the century, there was a feeling that females should avoid strenuous physicality, lest New Zealand become a land of 'muscular maidens'.

The woman's role was to prepare herself for motherhood and wifely duty, so to produce the stout sons who would protect the colony and Empire.

It would be a brave soul who claimed that chauvinism had eroded much by the 1950s. But the women of the Akarana Sporting Club in Auckland had their own ideas. Akarana was the thriving hub of a lively Maori sports scene, host to numerous hotly contested club games in various codes. The women who played hockey, softball and basketball were a new generation of urban Maori — Ngati Akarana — who lived in the central city before it was colonised by high-rise and motorway. They also worked. Jane Tehira (née Maxwell), a triple Silver Fern in hockey, basketball and softball, was a clothing factory-hand and her friend May Smith, a hockey Silver Fern in the 1950s, worked for a shoe manufacturer. They had always watched rugby and league, and saw no reason why they shouldn't give it a go themselves. At one match in Victoria Park a huge crowd watched a fast-moving, open game played by talented sportswomen wearing the men's borrowed jerseys. As Jane remembers, the women weren't very interested in the

The Akarana women's rugby team, in jerseys borrowed from the men, 1948, with Jane Maxwell (second from left, front) and May Smith (second from left, back).
Jane Tehira Collection

The spectators loved it . . .

65

scrummaging side of rugby, but wanted to run with the ball (they didn't much like the body contact, anyway, says May). The spectators loved it, and were particularly impressed by the ability of another team member, Violet Harrison, to kick goals from the sideline.

> It didn't seem the female thing to do at the time. It was a male dominated sport and it wasn't looked upon as a woman's sport then.
>
> *Jane Te Hira*

Men guarded their rugby domain jealously, of course. The inner sanctum of the after-match piss-up was generally barred to women (even if they had wanted to witness its unusual rites and rituals). As Doug Dalton said of his era, 'Women's role in rugby in those days was very small. You know, we used to have a lot of parties on Saturday night, where we had a keg. There were no women involved at all.' These practices were remarkably consistent, to the point of being highly regulated and coded forms of male bonding. 'I suppose people coming from another planet would think it was very uncouth,' says Neville McMillan. When wives and girlfriends were re-admitted to the circle, usually some time after nine o'clock, back at someone's house, the gender barrier stayed up. 'They would arrive and much of your time was spent around the keg in the kitchen where the guys spoke,' says 1960s All Black John Graham. 'The girls sat in the lounge and I don't know what they did really! When the keg emptied you went home. It was pretty basic.'

When the keg emptied you went home. It was pretty basic.

Even so, memories of such sub-bacchanalian delights are not without their tinges of nostalgia. In his 1976 excoriation of the New Zealand psyche, *The Passionless People*, Gordon McLauchlan wrote, 'I can remember the post-football beer parties on Saturday nights in the 1950s, the main source of entertainment . . . The most prized guests were All Blacks but there were too few of those to go around. So Dads reliving adolescent dreams had to do. They and you were allowed to get "a bit full", just enough to subdue reality and let sentimentality wash over the group in tales of past rugby glories, of famous games seen and players met, and of humorous drunken escapades, and, if the company was "adult" enough, of the prodigious "rooting" of anonymous girls, the unknown daughters and sisters of unknown non-sportsmen . . . They were childish, unreal affairs, but I look back at some of them with genuine warmth and gratitude. Outside our own families they were the only close and emotional relationships any of us had.'

For the women who had grown accustomed to the chivalrous behaviour of well-heeled American GIs during the war, the return of traditional New Zealand courtship rituals must have been somewhat disappointing. If so, they got used to it. Not until 1983 did players' wives and partners win the right to attend Ranfurly Shield after-match functions at Lancaster Park in Christchurch. Until then they had been offered tea and scones in a separate room, while the men attended to the serious business of dissecting the game over a table of beers and sausage rolls.

> When early matches were advertised in the local newspapers, the ads would say things like 'ladies free'. And the term would always be 'ladies'. A woman could go along and be a spectator at a male sport, which of course women continue to be through the twentieth century. That's one of the things that male sport always does. It makes women spectators of the male body and male space.
>
> *sociologist Caroline Daly*

KICKING FOR TOUCH

Is it ironic then, that at the time of rugby's greatest influence, New Zealand played some of its dourest rugby? How did a people determined to savour the fruits of peace after war turn their national game into such a grim business? Was it just the natural sporting expression of a stolid suburban ethos, or did the old play-to-win philosophy simply preclude the sheer risk of running it wide? It was a paradox, observed one writer, 'that a Calvinistic heritage, rigidly opposed to public displays and a recognition of emotional contacts, should discover its self-image in the extravagant and dramatic and expressive contact sport of rugby'. Maybe New Zealanders wanted the best of both worlds. But if the style of play was a clue to the national character, it was also undoubtedly a response to the crushing four-nil defeat of the All Blacks by the Springboks in South Africa in 1949.

> I think you'd have to blame the 1949 Springboks for that dourness because their forward play was far stronger and more advanced than New Zealand's. In fact, a rugby correspondent told me that New Zealand's forward play was so deficient in the early stages that Danie Craven actually came to the hotel and settled down the All Black pack and gave them some instructions on scrummaging. I'm sure rugby historians will curse me for mentioning it! But that is true.
>
> It was also part of the aftermath of the war. I was just entering my youthful manhood at that time and the country was so dull. Well, to a young man it was dull. But to the older men returning from the war, they wanted peace and quiet and serenity. My generation literally took to its heels, went overseas

I think you'd have to blame the 1949 Springboks for that dourness . . .

67

to seek the excitement and stimulation there. It wasn't in New Zealand.

So it may be that rugby didn't feel any demand upon it to be anything but dour, and to apply the lessons they'd learnt from the dour Afrikaaners in 1949.

Ian Cross

I never have ever had fun at rugby football. I've had a lot of satisfaction out of succeeding at it and playing well at it. But I've often been asked, what was the most enjoyable moment, or enjoyable game. And I said, well, I never had one. It was satisfaction out of the result or performing well myself. Disappointment if it was the other way.

Bob Scott

There may well have been logical tactical reasons for the dullness of New Zealand rugby, but it's hard to avoid the conclusion that New Zealanders also considered the hard-slogging game a virtue, not a vice. Sandra Coney quotes her father, Tom Pearce, who loomed large as a selector, coach and manager in Auckland (and national) rugby in the 1950s and 60s. 'What is this bright open rugby

The haircuts, the hats, the fags in the mouths — the uniform face of rugby in the 1950s.
NZ Herald

[but] the froth on the beer, the icing on the cake . . . It is a long time since we have seen eight Auckland forwards surging forward to the kill with backs speeding behind them. Until we do, Auckland rugby will have all the glitter and glamour of a modern jerry-built house on a rotten foundation.' Spectators who cheered open, entertaining rugby, wrote Pearce, wanted 'merely the glamour of the game without the meat'. Beer, meat, kill — the defining metaphors of post-war rugby. If there was one defining figure, it was Colin Earl Meads, who towered over New Zealand rugby like a pinetree from the late 1950s to the early 1970s. Physically huge, massively strong, a brilliant forward and an uncompromising competitor, Meads was once described by the great fullback Fergie McCormick as 'a terrible man with the silver fern on'. It was noble savagery, and New Zealanders identified with it.

> There's a story that's told of a little back country church in the King Country, and the words up there in letters of fire on the side of the church, 'If Jesus Christ came to the King Country tomorrow, what would you do?' And somebody had written underneath, 'Play him at lock and put Colin Meads on the side of the scrum.' Colin Meads and Jesus Christ! Very important. He represented physically, I think, that type of the New Zealander. Strong as a bull, didn't talk much, kept his talking for the rugby field, expressed himself physically by and large. I came to the point where Colin Meads represented

me as well. I would have liked to have been as strong and as gifted and as totally remorseless as Colin Meads. Some are called, few are chosen.

Ian Fraser

The suppression of pain is absolutely fundamental to the male stereotype in New Zealand. And again, that emerged out of a colonial frontier experience where suppressing pain was important. People lived in pretty tough situations, they were often a long way from doctors, so it was actually functional. And as you get to an urban society, rugby was a way of keeping alive that suppression of pain. The essence of a good rugby player is someone who is utterly oblivious to pain.

Jock Phillips

I was hopeless at playing rugby, absolutely hopeless. Humiliated, fat, pushed around, useless . . . It defined you. I was in the same year at school as Waka Nathan and Mac Herewini. I saw three of my classmates play at Twickenham in 1967. Gosh, it defined me all right. I saw them get the glory while I was picking up the scraps on detention.

David Lange

I can remember sleeping out overnight, queuing for tickets at Athletic Park with my father. And of course it always poured with rain. There was a lot of beer drunk. There was a great sort of sharing and parties and food and a lot of ritual preparation. And you stayed there and you got cramp and you got soaked and then about ten o'clock I guess, they let you into the ground and you sat there with all the food and beer and so on. And you watched three incredibly boring curtain-raisers where the ground was completely churned up. And then you got your main game at three o'clock. And in the style of the fifties the games were always very dour. Crash, bang stuff, up and down the touch line. And you went through that and you got colder and colder as the afternoon wore on and then it ended and there was this huge exodus. And you walked down the hill in a great mass of people, and by that stage, if you were a kid, you were tired and you were ratty. But you didn't dare show it because it was meant to be the great day. The great ritual.

journalist Tony Reid

. . . in the style of the fifties the games were always very dour. Crash, bang stuff . . .

The other great ritual came from the wireless. Winston McCarthy, who became the disembodied voice of rugby for several generations of New Zealanders, began his commentating career on the Kiwis tour immediately after the war, where his famous catch-cry — 'Listen . . . listen . . . it's a goal' — was born. Huddled around radios in kitchens, living rooms, on farms or on work sites, rugby fans had to accept that what McCarthy related was indeed what was happening on the field. McCarthy's exuberant style turned rugby into melodrama, a heightened experience that, for the length it took to play a game of football, transported listeners to another place. There was no television. Anyone not at the ground saw the game through McCarthy's eyes. It was, quite literally, a vision shared.

> We had the radio commentaries to listen to and the transference of Winston McCarthy coming out of the radio and into our minds. So we had all the games in our mind's eye. And that's a very potent thing to do, when you burn the image of games into the mind. People of my age now can still remember the games, where they were, who they were with, who scored the tries, what it smelt like, what it felt like. All the drama is still etched into our brain cells.
>
> *journalist Warwick Roger*

> I was two teams of fifteen people, and I played myself, or we played our-selves, in my grandmother's backyard. Which was fairly difficult because they had a revolving clothesline in the middle, and it was small. And I was both teams, and I kicked back and forth, and I tackled, and I did things, and I scored in the corners — and I never knew how the game would go. I also gave an extremely loud commentary on the game, where I out-Winstoned McCarthy. Although, I was probably several Winstons short of a McCarthy.
>
> *Tony Reid*

One man's vision shared by many. The immortal Winston McCarthy relaying the game to a nation, 1961.
Radio New Zealand
Sound Archives

1956 AND ALL THAT

As soon as I was old enough to be allowed to wander outside the house on the street, I observed a rectangular world. All the kids in the street were playing on the front lawn. That was the first rugby pitch I saw. And then at school there was the three-quarter-length field, the goal posts, the dental clinic in the corner.

writer Lloyd Jones

In 1956, Lloyd Jones's rectangular world was being built. Huge demand for housing after the war prompted a construction boom. State tenants could buy their houses now. The 'Kiwi dream' of home ownership conjured suburbs out of empty space. The welfare state was there if you got into trouble, just as you could kick for touch on the rugby field. It was a conformist society, and a conformist game. New Zealanders hugged the sidelines of life, inching toward their goals with gritty determination. They were easily excited, though. When the new wave of American cultural imperialism broke over the cities and towns, creating a minor cult of bodgies, widgies and milk bar cowboys, the old wowserism was manifested in mild moral panics. In 1956, Johnny Devlin heard his first Elvis

Presley record. Before the decade was out, he was the country's first rock 'n' roll star.

Soon, rugby's grip would loosen. A new generation would rebel against the blanketing conformity of the suburb and the safe mores of their parents. But in 1956, rugby came about as close as a game could to defining a moment in time. Seven years on from the Dunkirk of '49, another Springbok team arrived in New Zealand. It became a national campaign to redeem New Zealand rugby.

> It was revenge for '49. It was exceptionally hard. I think there would have been people in some of those games who would have been prepared to die for Waikato, or die for Auckland.
>
> *Warwick Roger*

They were the enemy all right, but the mighty Boks were also tremendously alluring. For all the alleged dreariness of the country, it was a romantic era. A

Strangers from a strange land. 1956 Springboks Jappie Bekker, Clive Ulyate and Harry Newtown Walker delight teenagers at the Timaru Scottish Society's weekly dance.
NZ Herald

young queen and her prince had only recently visited to a rapturous welcome, and New Zealanders had flocked to the Hollywood movies of Marilyn Monroe, Grace Kelly, Gregory Peck and Cary Grant, heroines and heroes of a hopeful time. The South Africans were familiar and exotic at the same time, a bit like movie stars. Crowds gathered just to view them waving from hotel balconies. In New Plymouth, there was great excitement — Taranaki held the Ranfurly Shield and were deemed very worthy opponents. A huge parade down Devon Street on the morning of the match, complete with a hospital plane bearing the legend 'Jo'burg or bust', drew most of the town to watch. Among them was a quiet and studious teenager named Judy Russell, who later went to the park with her father to see the Springboks play.

> *. . . it was a romantic era.*

> I remember being greatly excited, because I thought that [Basie] Viviers was absolutely wonderful. And he turned around and I was quite sure he smiled at me — sure he looked straight at me and smiled! So that really made my day. I don't remember very much about the game, but I do remember that.
>
> *Judy Russell*

By the time of the fourth and last test in Auckland, the All Blacks were ahead two-one. South Africa could still square the series. Eden Park was packed to capacity and beyond. The Springboks had not lost a series in 60 years.

> The main concern was whether you were actually going to see anything. Because we were on banana boxes, the main concern was to stay upright and wonder what on earth would happen if you fell off the banana box, because you'd just disappear. My abiding memory of '56 is being very close to where [All Black] Tiny White was kicked in the fourth test. The action happened right down in front of where we were, and I think — I imagine — I can still hear Tiny White scream out in agony as the boots went into him. I certainly have a very vivid memory of the ambulance men coming onto the field, and a couple of policemen stationing themselves to make sure the crowd didn't come onto the field as well.
>
> *Warwick Roger*

Elsewhere in the crowd sat the young Gavin Cormack, son of the man who had erected a temporary stand for the game. The Cormack family were seated directly in front of the official party, containing the New Zealand Union representatives and Dr and Mrs Danie Craven. When All Black forward Peter Jones gathered the ball 40 yards from the South African line, everyone around young Gavin had to stand to see the resulting try that would clinch the game and the series. 'My mother was pushed down by Mrs Craven, who couldn't see, and probably wasn't very pleased that the try was going to be scored anyway,' Cormack remembers. Jones's after-match comment that he was 'absolutely buggered', broadcast over the park's sound system and on the radio, sent a delayed ripple of laughter around the crowd, and around a country that normally went purse-lipped at such locker-room language.

> There is a famous photograph of Danie Craven more or less conceding victory, and a sea of faces in front of the old members' stand. And everyone looks as miserable as sin. They were stunned. They had waited seven years for this, and had finally beaten the old enemy, and there is not a happy face amongst them. They're all wearing the same hats, the same expressions. That photograph tells me quite a lot about the New Zealand I grew up in. It was not an unhappy place, but it was a place of great sameness. And rugby was part of that sameness.
>
> *Warwick Roger*

As the 1950s receded, that sameness began to lift too. In some ways, rugby had become so all-consuming precisely because there was very little else to do or watch. The jet age and television would change that, and the children of the baby boom — the ones whose formative years were spent queuing overnight for test match tickets or perched on their fathers' shoulders to see a game — would find other diversions. The old tribal rituals could never hold the undivided attention of a generation that came of age in the cultural crucible of the 1960s. Where the suburbs had once been a place to find refuge, they were now a place to leave — in some cases to flee. Rugby could not be 'religion and desire and fulfilment all in one' forever.

The Springbok tour of 1956 was like a high tide . . .

The Springbok tour of 1956 was like a high tide: at the moment of rugby's apotheosis it began to fall away again. This isn't to say that the game ceased to capture the collective imagination of a country, or that sensational games and tours didn't take place from that point on. Only that there would be other things on the minds of New Zealanders. The simple joys of rugby would be inevitably compromised by an increasingly complex world. And it would be in the supreme rivalry with South Africa that New Zealand would finally see the other side of its national game. The Springboks were there for the best of times, and they would also be there for the worst.

13.
Far from the televised hype of big city rugby, members of the East Coast team watch a junior match before their third division game against Buller at Rangitukia, near the East Cape, 1995.

14.
Barefoot, brown-skinned, white-skinned: since rugby began in New Zealand it has been an important mixer of men — and boys. Rangitukia, East Coast.

15.
The face of local rugby? The East Coast pack warms up before the game with Buller.

16.
A few hands on the way up the coast from Gisborne. The Buller team, from the opposite corner of New Zealand, are as white as the East Coast team is brown. Not that anyone is really interested in things like that when the boys take the field.

17.
The grave of the great George Nepia, just off the roadside at Rangitukia, with the distant goalposts of his beloved football ground just visible to the left. The Buller team may not be familiar with everything around these parts, but everyone knows the Nepia name.

18.
*Watching the match.
They call the balcony
'the corporate box',
although at last
inspection there was
no sign of a courtesy
fridge. On the wall
inside the changing
rooms nearby hangs a
sign: 'This is a dope
free club. If you want
to smoke dope, do it at
your club.'*

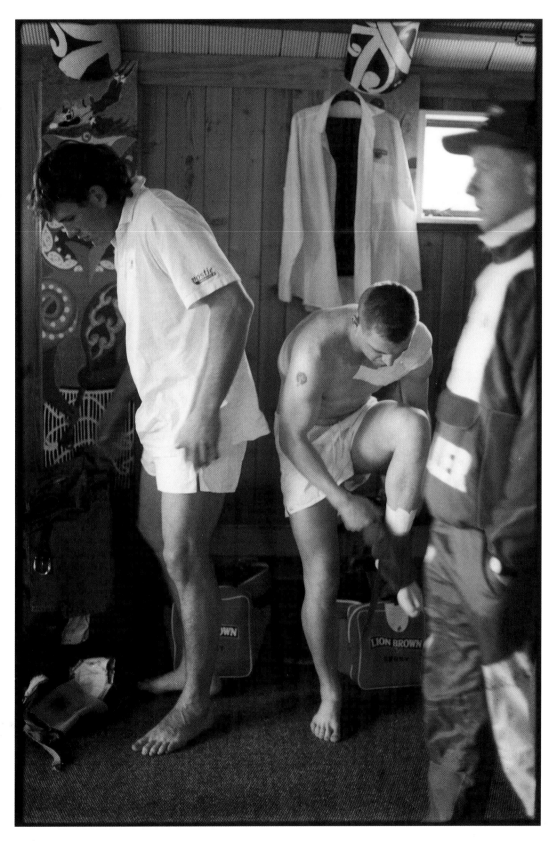

19.
*Rugby the Maori way:
the Buller team takes
over the whare tipuna
for its changing room
before the match. 'To
spook them,' one of the
East Coast team said,
laughing.*

20.
The East Coast clubrooms (complete with Bryan Williams caricature), and the gate at the Rangitukia ground: where white and brown, home and away, meet and mingle on the common ground of rugby.

Part 3

THE PATH TO '81

South Africa is the only other country that thinks about rugby like we do, and looks upon it as an intellectual exercise, something which you'll sit down and analyse, and analyse for fun. Other countries play it, but they don't live it like New Zealand and South Africa.

cartoonist Murray Ball

The love of rugby shared by New Zealand and South Africa was, for much of the twentieth century, a bond that reached across distance and difference to join two peoples. Geographically and historically separated, they were one in their passion for the game. And yet, in this very unity, there was division. In the love of rugby, there were the seeds of hatred. Largely because of rugby, the struggle for justice in a foreign land would become a painful part of history in New Zealand.

In 1981 the civil war in South Africa spilled over, in a strange and convoluted way, onto the streets of New Zealand. The consequences were so appalling, so vivid, that the event is now commonly referred to only by its barest chronological label: '81. What it meant for New Zealand is still not entirely clear, other than that at the centre of a defining moment in modern New Zealand history stood the country's national game. A team from another land visited, they played their matches, and they left. It lasted only a couple of months, but New Zealand was altered by it.

People have asked why so many New Zealanders were so incensed by sporting contact with South Africa; why no similar protest over ping pong with China, why no comparable outrage over Pol Pot's atrocities or Indonesian human rights? After all, there have been and still are regimes as evil as South Africa's at the height of apartheid. The answer is surely obvious. New Zealand didn't play rugby with those countries. Only rugby carried the implicit imprimatur of the entire nation. Only the All Blacks purported to represent all New Zealanders. Only rugby meant more than just a game.

For all the same reasons that rugby could unite a country, or at least captivate

Tries and Penalties

the imaginations of a large proportion of its inhabitants, it could divide and disillusion them. Rugby could only take New Zealand so low because it had taken it so high in the past. And so the story of rugby's dark side begins with everything that's good about the game.

COMMON GROUND

Rangitukia, near the very tip of the North Island's rugged and isolated East Cape, is a typical rural Maori community. A collection of houses and small farms, backed onto by big hill-country stations, it lies five kilometres down a dusty road from the larger but still tiny Tikitiki. On a cold, wet winter's Saturday, this tiny hamlet plays host to a third division match between two of the least successful teams in the competition — East Coast, the home union, and Buller, from the opposite corner of the country on the West Coast of the South Island.

It's a game that emblemises everything rugby has meant to New Zealand: home and away, north and south, Maori and Pakeha. Buller is as white a team as East Coast is brown. Rugby has brought them together, as it has been doing for the races since Maori took to the game with such verve and enthusiasm in the 1870s.

The Buller team is welcomed with all the hospitality accorded any visitors. The local marae becomes the South Islanders' base camp and changing room. After the match, there will be a feast, for which preparations have been underway since the day began. Marae and rugby club merge. This is rugby the Maori way.

The match is also the week's big event for those who come to watch; a mini-jamboree in a place where not a lot happens beyond the steady routines of farming. On the East Coast, rugby is far more than just a game or a pastime. It's the centre of social life in winter, a genuine force that binds the scattered little communities that dot the hinterland between Gisborne and Opotiki. This has never been more true than since the economic revolution of the 1980s and 90s put the region into permanent recession, increased unemployment and reduced welfare payments. Rugby, at least, is something to get excited about.

It is also the object of great pride on the Coast, the birthplace of many All Blacks and great Maori players. Often they made their names playing for other provinces. Only two have come from the East Coast Union itself. Within sight of the goalposts on this little rural rugby ground lies the grave of one of them — and the greatest of them all — George Nepia.

Nepia was actually born further south, at Wairoa in Poverty Bay, in 1905 —

It's a game that emblemises everything rugby has meant to New Zealand.

the year the first official All Black team toured Britain. He moved to Rangitukia to marry his beloved Ngati Porou wife, Huinga, with whom he is buried, across the road from their little house where their daughter Kiwi now lives. His old tractor stands by the front gate. Way back down the road is the little chapel at Tikitiki where George and Huinga were married. Outside the church is a memorial to another great son of the Coast, Apirana Ngata. While Ngata was alive, George would often ride his horse across the Waiapu River to the statesman's house, 'The Bungalow', to play tennis. Just beyond Nepia's grave is another little churchyard with a gateway carved by his son Oma in tribute to his father. On the right-hand pillar a figure holding a rugby ball is inscribed, simply, 'George'.

Locals will tell you that European tourists have made the pilgrimage here, miles from the usual holiday trails, to the home of George Nepia. In its own way, the rough rural paddock on which Buller and East Coast slog it out is as much hallowed turf as Eden Park, Ellis Park or Twickenham. George spent the best part of his life playing (for his old club Rangers), coaching or refereeing here. And every Christmas he would play host to a member or two of his most famous team, the 1924 'Invincibles'. His foster son Jim Perry remembers the children listening from behind doors or outside windows to tales of that triumphant rugby tour.

Nepia was only 19 when he played fullback in every game of the unbeaten series in Britain. He was hailed at home and abroad as a hero, a genius of the game, 'the last line of defence', revered for his prodigious kicking and fearless tackling. But he became much more than a sporting celebrity. In the 1920s, New Zealand truly wanted to believe in racial harmony. A generation that could remember the land wars of the previous century was still alive. There was an idealism — however flawed or patronising — that encouraged a belief in brotherhood. Nepia, so young and so gifted, became a symbol for the time. Here was a country whose first sporting superstar could be a young Maori from the backblocks.

George Nepia, 1957, accustomed to victory on the rugby field, but unable to triumph over the policy of his own rugby union.
Alexander Turnbull Library

Nepia, so young and so gifted, became a symbol for the time.

> It seems to me that in terms of the developing national myth, Nepia has a number of great advantages. He was a Maori, and he lived so long. In the creation of sporting myths and legends, that's a very great advantage. He epitomises so much about the 1920s. A young Maori in a society which, above all else I think, was becoming convinced that race relations in New Zealand could be much better than they had in the past. A real genuine belief that New Zealand could put together an egalitarian society which involved Maori people as well as Pakeha.
>
> *Len Richardson*

It was a noble ideal, but it was also to some extent a sentimental conceit. Just how prepared New Zealanders were, not only to treat Maori equally, but to defend that equality, would be tested soon after Nepia's 1924 triumph. In 1928 the New Zealand Rugby Football Union received its first invitation to tour South Africa — the newest, but rapidly becoming the greatest, rugby rival. Nepia, along with other Maori players of the day, was denied the opportunity of playing in South Africa against the Springboks. Apartheid had not yet become a formal system of oppression, but its foundations were well in place. Nepia was an early — but not the first — casualty of a tangled cord of race, rugby and politics that had bound New Zealand to South Africa since before he was born.

UNWISE DECISIONS

At the turn of the century New Zealand was locked in the imperial embrace of Great Britain. The 'mother country' was still home to most, and was even thought of as such by many Maori; members of the Natives Tour wrote about 'going home' on their incredible rugby journey in 1888. Within the Empire, however, there was competition for the rewards of Mother England's attention, and no politician of the era competed harder than Richard Seddon. When Britain went to war with the Dutch Afrikaaners in South Africa, he seized the opportunity to offer troops and display loyalty.

Maori certainly wanted to fight for New Zealand, and they trained for battle. But this was to be a white man's war; brown allies in such an escapade were unthinkable in the logic of the age (although some took advantage of European surnames and facial features, and volunteered successfully). The last stages of the Boer War coincided with the coronation of Edward VII, and a Maori contingent travelled to the celebrations in England on the same ship as the New Zealand 10th Contingent, on its way to fight in South Africa. Stopping in Durban, they were photographed in the streets being transported by African bearers. It

The Maori contingent for the coronation of Edward VII, which stopped in South Africa on the way to London, 1902. Canterbury Museum

was as close as they got to any fighting before sailing on to London. This was the first South African field from which Maori would be excluded.

Only three years later, in 1905, Seddon found his companion-piece for the imperial trophy cabinet. The great 'Originals' who introduced the term All Black and who lost only one game on their epic tour of Britain and France, became symbols not only of what a good clean colonial upbringing could do for a man, but of what a 'white race' could achieve. Seddon saw the apron strings of Mother England as a safeguard of 'racial purity, and the maintaining of a nation worthy of the representatives they sent home to uphold the national game'. Yes, there were Maori in the team. But Seddon's words were symptomatic of a general hysteria over sustaining a far-flung, sparsely populated empire.

The trinity of rugby, race and war would come together a decade later. The First World War found New Zealanders playing rugby wherever they fought. Maori — who were permitted to fight this time — were no exception. There was intense rivalry within the battalion for rugby honours in the inter-company competitions and for places in the New Zealand divisional team that contested the King's Cup with other allied teams. On the one occasion that no Maori was in the divisional side, a young Maori corporal came onto the field to lead them in the pre-game haka. Maori and things Maori were part of the New Zealand self-image.

Vice-captain of the New Zealand Services team that won the King's Cup was

Maori and things Maori were part of the New Zealand self-image.

a young man named Ranji Wilson. A gifted loose forward and a pre-war All Black, he was part West Indian on his mother's side. His proper name was Nathaniel Arthur Wilson, but his ethnic background earned him his nickname. It also earned him a less affectionate label. When the victorious Services team was invited to play in South Africa on its way home from Europe, Wilson was 'classified' as 'coloured'. For the first time in what would be a long and painful history, a New Zealander was excluded from a New Zealand team because of the colour of his skin.

> The invitation to the New Zealand army team was extended by the South African Rugby Board to call in to South Africa to play a series of games on the way home. And according to two members of the army team who spoke to my late co-author [R H Chester], South African officers who were in England at the time and South Africans who had played in the King's Cup, suggested that it would be 'unwise' — that was the word they used — to take him to South Africa. So they decided to go without him.
>
> *Neville McMillan*

> That was the one rugby story my grandfather ever told me. He was on board that ship coming back from World War One and it was put about that Ranji Wilson was not to be allowed to play because he was a coloured person. My grandfather thought that was sufficient reason to stay on board as well, which he did! And I think that awakened in me as a young boy of about nine or ten, this sense that something was clearly wrong about South African rugby if they wouldn't let Ranji Wilson play.
>
> *Len Richardson*

Brown and white alike play rugby during World War I, Fontaine 1918.
RSA Collection, Alexander Turnbull Library

We made a mistake allowing them to dictate like that. The same as they did in 1928 and again in 1949. If we'd have put our foot down and said, well, no, we tour under our own conditions and not yours, then I think all this problem that came later might not have arisen.

Neville McMillan

We made a mistake allowing them to dictate like that.

Between Ranji Wilson's exclusion and George Nepia missing the1928 tour to South Africa, the Springboks made their first visit to New Zealand. The 1921 series was the official beginning of what would become one of the most intense international rivalries in any sport. It was also another early clue for New Zealanders to the character of their chosen football foe.

Unable to dictate conditions this time, the Springboks faced a full Maori side in Napier. The tourists won a tough, close match, with its fair share of grudge and grind. George Nepia described the atmosphere in his autobiography: 'This was more than rugby, it was a racial conflict.' But it was nothing compared to events off the field. A South African correspondent cabled home a report that so horrified an anonymous Post Office worker that he leaked its contents to the local *Napier Daily Telegraph*.

'This was the most unfortunate match ever played . . . It was bad enough having to play a team officially designated "New Zealand Natives", but the spectacle of thousands of Europeans frantically cheering on a band of coloured men to defeat members of their own race was too much for the Springboks, who were frankly disgusted.'

Horrified too were New Zealanders when they read their papers that day. The South African team manager, Harold Bennett, carefully distanced himself from the telegram and its sentiments. But he would later suggest that future Springbok sides would not play Maori, and that no Maori would be welcome in South Africa. New Zealand was starting to learn that while rugby was the common ground, there was much separating the two countries.

Part of the difference can be traced to the way rugby took hold in each society. South Africa always mirrored the English experience more closely, with an urban, moneyed class taking to the game. New Zealand quickly made rugby a great leveller, an opportunity for Jack to pack down with his master, a game for both races. This phenomenon was not lost on the custodians of the game in England, who in the early years of the twentieth century commented on the greater social acceptability of touring South Africans, as opposed to the plebeians of New Zealand rugger. This view held even as South African rugby began to draw

The New Zealand Maoris who lost to the Springboks in 1921 and who caused their opponents such racial anguish.
Hocken Library

its players more from the Afrikaaner middle class and less from the colonial English upper class. It was always felt the Springboks played a straighter game, the kind of game the English knew, rather than the tactically dubious New Zealand game, with its innovations like the wing forward and its emphasis on winning, not merely playing.

So rugby reflected difference and similarity. The attitude of the South Africans was offensive, yes. But rugby was by now more important than theories about domestic race relations, let alone the racial politics of a strange land far away. Just as South Africa wished, no Maori would play for the All Blacks in South Africa for another 50 years. And the whistle-blowing Post Office clerk in Napier lost his job.

NO MAORIS — NO TOUR

If there is a high point in New Zealand's passionate identification with rugby it is 1956, which heralded another Springbok tour in a sporting relationship that by now consumed public attention. Memories of the All Blacks' disastrous defeat in South Africa in 1949 were strong. If New Zealanders had any qualms about playing a racially selected side, they were swept away in the collective desire to atone for past losses. But at the very moment of unity in victory, society was poised on the brink of change. Rugby would never again hold such sway as it did during that one winter, and New Zealanders would never again turn away as one from the injustice of playing South Africans on their own racist terms.

The years since 1921 had seen the regular exclusion of great Maori players from South African tours — stars of the game who might ordinarily have gained automatic selection for All Black teams. In 1928, George Nepia and Jimmy Mill stayed at home. Who knows? Maybe the two-all series draw that year would have been a win if New Zealand had fielded their strongest side. Nepia, who would later take part in protests about the policy of exclusion, confined his criticisms to the sporting logic rather than to the morality of playing it South Africa's way.

> I think he always felt that the New Zealand teams were not true New Zealand teams if they didn't have the best players in them. And in those cases, with people like himself and [fellow 1924 Invincible] Lui Paewai, and other greats who were excluded from teams that went to South Africa, it hurt him a lot internally. I heard him speaking in later years about that disappointment and how he along with other people fought for years to get the New Zealand Rugby Union to change their attitude towards accepting that edict from South Africa that no Maoris should be included.
>
> *Jim Perry*

Over the years a justification had evolved within the rugby administration that the policy of exclusion was in the best interests of Maori. By sending all-white teams to South Africa, it was argued, New Zealand was not acquiescing to a racist creed, but rather protecting its respected fellow citizens from the humiliation and injustice they might encounter in the racist republic.

> They decided that it wouldn't be fair to the Maori to expose them to what might happen to them in South Africa — ridicule, treatment as second-class citizens. And that was the prevailing attitude right through 1928, 1949, 1960. They were trying to do the right thing by Maori — I think wrongly — but at least their hearts were in the right place.
>
> *Ron Palenski*

If the policy was born out of compassion, it could sometimes be applied without any great regard for the feelings of the players concerned. Just before the outbreak of the Second World War another South African tour was planned. One of the great Maori players of the day was Everard Jackson, who had been first selected in 1936 to play Australia, and had played against the Springboks

83

when they visited in 1937. He was Ngati Porou, educated at Te Araroa Native School and Rerekohu District High School on the East Coast, a product of the Depression of the 20s and 30s. Rugby was his passport to the world, but not to South Africa.

> I know one of the saddest times of his life was when he played for the North Island shortly before the war, and then, together with other Maori players of his generation who played in either the North Island or the South Island teams, was quietly, without anything actually being said directly about the reasons for it, shunted home because there was to be a trial for a tour of South Africa. And it was understood and accepted by the administration that they, as Maori players, could not go. And he thought that was one of the most demeaning and insulting periods of his life.
>
> *Syd Jackson*

The tour for which Jackson was not considered was called off. War broke out in Europe and conventional international rugby was suspended. Despite the history of mutual animosity, South Africa entered the Second World War (as

The All Blacks for the second test against the Springboks, Lancaster Park, 1937, with Everard Jackson (centre, back row), Tom Pearce (third from right, back) and Doug Dalton, (second from right, back).
NZ Rugby Museum

they had in the First World War) on the British side. Once again, New Zealanders — including Maori — fought alongside their rugby opponents. Captain Everard Jackson served in the Maori Battalion and was severely injured in the Western Desert campaign, losing a leg. After the war, Everard lived in almost constant pain and endured countless operations before his death in 1975. His son remembers him as one who never spoke much about the past, but who harboured considerable bitterness about Maori participation in the Second World War, believing they had been duped by propaganda into believing they were fighting for a better world in which their children could grow up. Apirana Ngata had believed that participation in war would be the key to full citizenship. This was not Everard Jackson's experience of post-war New Zealand, despite his pride in the achievements of the Maori Battalion.

When the All Blacks toured South Africa in 1949, again there were no Maori in the team. Having proved themselves conquering heroes in war, they could still not conquer a state of mind that held rugby with the Springboks above the dignity of one's own people. This was not an era of dissent or protest, but the odd voice could be heard above the roar of the rugby crowd. On being advised that such a tour would take place, Major-General Sir Howard Kippenberger responded in 1948, 'I had Maoris under my command for two years, and in that time they had 1500 casualties, and I'm not going to acquiesce to any damned Afrikaaner's saying they cannot go. To hell with them.' The South African newspaper *Die Burger* took exception, arguing that the exclusion of Maori was indeed for their own good, 'for we cannot imagine that they would find the tour of the Union enjoyable'. Kippenberger apologised and withdrew his comments.

Rugby's high tide in 1956 began to recede in the following years. Of course it remained the national game, the one sure way of stopping the national clock for a couple of hours on a Saturday. But the blanketing conformity of the 1950s was lifting. The grim, muddy struggle of fifteen men in black could no longer articulate everybody's idea of who we were or wanted to be. The post-war urbanisation of New Zealand was in full swing. Auckland was sprawling north and west, houses going up in new subdivisions, nappies drying on a forest of washing lines.

Maori were particularly mobile. Veterans of the 28th Maori Battalion had already moved in large numbers to the cities in search of work, spearheading an internal relocation described as 'not so much a "drift" as an irreversible migration in search of work' in one government report. In the years after 1950, a full 75 per cent of Maori would leave their rural homes and put down new roots in

. . . the blanketing conformity of the 1950s was lifting.

85

the towns and cities of the North Island. Maori adapted fast, intermarriage with Pakeha increased and a form of pan-tribalism began to emerge as traditional social structures were applied to the new setting. Sports clubs — and rugby — were part of this simultaneous integration and affirmation of cultural identity, with clubs like Akarana in Auckland becoming community centres for inner-city Maori.

Pakeha, on the other hand, were generally confused by the changing place of Maori people in society, and the debate about sporting contact with South Africa reflected this. When the 1960 All Black tour was farewelled at Parliament, team manager Tom Pearce said the decision not to take Maori players 'sprang only from love of the Maoris, these gentle people. We wouldn't hurt them in the least.' This kind of paternalism was compounded by a current belief that Maori were an innately superior race to black Africans, a theme which South African rugby boss Dr Danie Craven had examined in a 1959 speech based on 'profound anthropological studies'. It was a theme supported by our own rugby administrators, including a former Rugby Union president Henry Blazey (brother of Ces), who said nearly ten years after Craven's remarks, 'You must realise that our Maoris are three hundred years ahead of the South African native.'

White New Zealanders had little difficulty empathising, therefore, with the

Former rugby adversaries on the field, united now in their determination to maintain sporting contacts. Tom Pearce, former All Black, pillar of Auckland rugby and national selector and manager, here with Dr Danie Craven during the 1956 Springbok tour.
NZ Herald

paternalistic echoes from South Africa. The Dutch-born South African president, Hendrik Verwoerd, justified the banning of a racially inclusive All Black tour in 1966 on the grounds that Maori staying in white hotels in white areas, playing with and against white men on the rugby field, would encourage black and coloured South Africans to want the same. Maori themselves were not unanimously opposed to white-only All Black tours, and were as likely to dismiss the question of apartheid as their Pakeha neighbours. When the Springboks toured in 1965, the Maori Council announced it would not protest, since 'the Maori people love their rugby too much to allow a side issue to mar their enjoyment of the tour'.

It is too easy, then, to say that the Rugby Union's attitude to excluding Maori players was the product of genuine respect and concern, or even that it was based on misguided but well-meaning paternalism. There were indeed great gaps between New Zealand and South Africa in the attitudes of white settlers to the indigenous population, but there were certainly points of agreement too, including an unquestioning assumption of racial superiority, albeit expressed in different ways. Journalist Geoff Chapple described it as, 'Somewhere beneath the vaunt of racial equality, the everyday overcoming of the Maori race. Subtly done, or with state power as necessary — the police, the jails. New Zealand's sublime secret, and the chambers of that vibrated with silent sympathy for the white settler society in South Africa.'

New Zealand's sublime secret . . .

> I don't think for a moment that anybody, any thinking person, considered that the Rugby Union's edict had anything to do with protecting Maori. It was just a reflection, I believe, of the community's attitude towards Maori people in general — at that stage, to appease the attitudes of white South Africans.
>
> *Jim Perry*

FIRST PROTESTS

Against this montage of idealism, ignorance and condescension, a small movement opposed to official rugby policy began to grow. The Citizens' All Black Tour Association — CABTA — was a disparate group of predominantly European church members, trade unionists, teachers, students and the odd professional. Chairman and spokesman was Wellington surgeon Rolland O'Regan, married to a Maori, and father of Ngai Tahu leader, Sir Tipene O'Regan. Believing that New Zealanders weren't yet ready for the broader issue of human rights in South

. . . an unusually unanimous silence from both sides of the House.

Africa, the movement consciously focused its protest on the exclusion of Maori players, which, it was argued, was tantamount to importing apartheid into New Zealand: 'No Maoris — No Tour' was the slogan.

In early 1960, after the Rugby Union had refused to see the protest organisers, a deputation was made to the Prime Minister, Walter Nash, and the then acting opposition leader John Marshall. CABTA sought at the very least a pronouncement from the government against the tour, and no state farewell for the team. But they encountered an unusually unanimous silence from both sides of the House.

The beginnings of dissent. Protesters at Athletic Park, Wellington, disrupt the All Black trials, 1960.
News Media

It was an amazing deputation and interview. The atmosphere was electric. At one stage, in the middle of this meeting, the Maori members of the deputation broke into a haka in Nash's office. Nash couldn't be and wouldn't be moved. Marshall called us a bunch of agitators. Although one thing he said that was the least bit encouraging was that he didn't think the Rugby Union should ever let this happen again.

I don't think there is any doubt that the politicians thought that rugby was too big, too central to the lives of a lot of New Zealanders, really to buck the Rugby Union.

CABTA organiser David Stone

Marshall called us a bunch of agitators.

Walter Nash's refusal to publicly condemn the tour was seen by many, including his political supporters, as a failure to confront the issue on moral grounds, something the Prime Minister was normally not reluctant to do. His closest advisers within the public service had urged him to denounce the Union's decision, but Nash (who was a friend of Rugby Union chairman Cuth Hogg) actually defended it, saying 'it would be an act of the greatest folly and cruelty to the Maori race to allow their representatives to visit a country where colour is considered to be a mark of inferiority'. Nash's biographer Keith Sinclair wrote that while Nash had long denounced racism, he did not see that the issue of race in sport was becoming an international problem. However, on the team's return he did tell Hogg that the next tour must include Maori, or the invitation should clearly be to European players only, 'so that there will be no repetition of the unpleasantness over this tour'.

If New Zealand's homogeneous society could once have been relied on to smother any dissent on the subject of rugby with South Africa, there was now a clear divergence of views. Nearly 160,000 signatures were gathered in a nationwide petition, launched at a meeting in Wellington's town hall attended by more than 2000 people — including George Nepia (who sang for the crowd) and former commander of the Maori Battalion Lieutenant Colonel Arapeta Awatere. The latter reminded the audience that the last time he had marched had been under fire, fighting for the very rights now being denied Maori rugby players, all because some New Zealanders were 'gutless'.

The presence of war heroes among the protesters didn't stop the odd muttering within rugby circles that this was some insidious plot by rugby league in cahoots with the Communist Party. CABTA street stalls and meetings were watched by the newly formed New Zealand Security Service — the same government agency that had advised Nash that the controversy had only become so heated due to the Communists (as Sinclair put it, 'a secret insult to the intelligence and conscience of half the adult population').

Meanwhile, on a rugby pitch far from the corridors of power, the All Black trials were being disrupted for the first time ever by the direct action of protesters. For a young All Black on the brink of climbing his rugby Everest, it was profoundly confusing.

> Doubts certainly were placed in my mind about the rightness of going to South Africa. And that was shown by demonstrations at trial games, with people sitting on the grounds — quite unheard of in New Zealand rugby. And it certainly affected many of the players in the side, and I was deeply moved by it because I don't like seeing fellow New Zealanders being dragged forcibly off our fields.
>
> But there was a selfishness about me at that stage, and I suppose about the whole side. No team had gone since 1949. It was what you dreamed of as a New Zealander once you'd made the All Blacks – to go to South Africa.
>
> As we were flying out of the airport in Auckland, people ran out on to the tarmac. That was the most dramatic and unsettling event for all of us. It really did demonstrate the depth of feeling by a large number of New Zealanders — larger than we thought, by the way — in 1960, about the issue of social justice in another country.
>
> *former All Black John Graham*

By the time that plane left Whenuapai airport, South Africa's civil war had just begun. In March 1960, a peaceful protest against the pass law in Sharpeville township was turned into a bloodbath when security forces opened fire. Sixty-nine were shot dead, and 180 wounded. As South African journalist Allister Sparks wrote, 'Sharpeville was the turning point when black nationalist politics was outlawed, when it went underground and switched from strategies of nonviolence to those of guerrilla struggle. When what had been a civil rights campaign turned into a civil war of sorts . . . and South Africa started becoming a police state.'

How fitting, then, that the first All Black tour to be seriously challenged for its morality, should arrive not long after the blood had been washed from Sharpeville's streets. John Graham was aware of the massacre, and asked to be taken to the township — he was a history teacher as well as an All Black, and this was material for his classes in New Zealand. What he saw and photographed there, and in other rural ghetto areas, confirmed his earlier qualms about the tour. On his return, Graham spoke publicly about his experiences, and how they had confirmed his opposition to playing rugby with a country that oppressed its own population.

21.
The East Coast team hunkers down for the pre-game talk at the Waiapu Hotel. There are plans and strategies, of course, but rugby is unpredictable, and injury sidelines the best of them.

22.
After the match, the aftermatch. As one of the Buller team observes of East Coast hospitality, 'First they kill you with kindness, then they dick you.' Actually, it's the other way around . . .

23.
After the aftermatch, the speeches. The Buller captain pays tribute to his hosts.

24.
Rare jubilation in the East Coast changing room. Lurking near the bottom of the table they may be, but today they won! The player on the floor is a ring-in from Fiji.

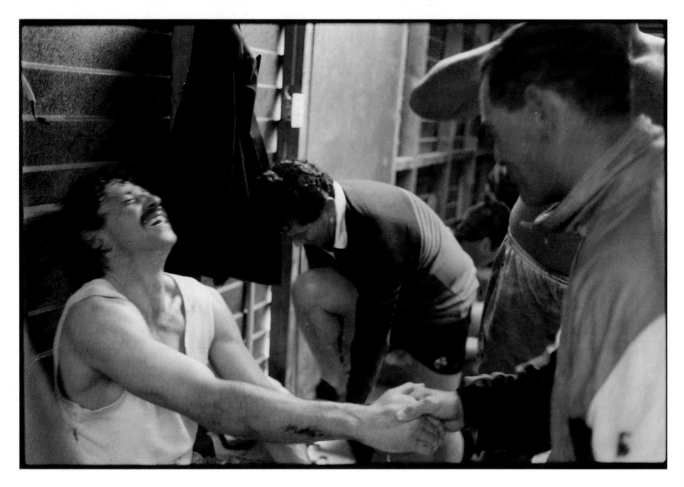

25.

Same as it ever was — the hard work starts here. These are the Wellington primary school representative trials in appalling conditions one afternoon at Athletic Park beneath the No 1 Stand. The team selected played in the southern North Island schools rugby tournament at Kilbirnie Park, Wellington. Meanwhile (below), two sisters watch the 1995 Wellington-Counties match in marginal conditions from the lofty heights of the Millard Stand.

26.
The club match, Avalon, Lower Hutt. The sights and sounds
haven't changed much since this was the only game in town, when
the local footy ground was the village well, and New Zealand slowed
to a standstill on winter afternoons. But times have changed.
Beyond these fields, the suburbs that once sustained the game are
home to a new generation, the corner shops are giving way to malls,
and the old television centre in the background is corporatised. For
now, the game goes on . . .

27.
In a previous era they might have trudged with their fathers to the big game, stood on wobbly beer crates to catch the action, and trudged home again with the faithful. Now these kids at a cinema complex in Auckland's Newmarket have a lot of alternatives. Below: a sign of the times – this is a women's rugby changing room.

I got into severe trouble with the Rugby Union and was told that under no circumstances could I repeat that speech – that in future I could speak about the rugby I played over there, and rugby players that I played against, but I was to make no more political comment whatsoever. That was quite a telling situation for a young fellow. I was gagged if you like.

John Graham

The CABTA protest arrives at Parliament, but the politicians were wary of upsetting the Rugby Union and its public.
News Media

The protest movement faded in the aftermath of the tour, but its impact would be felt before the decade was out. When South Africa invited another All Black tour for 1967, the issue of Maori inclusion was top of the agenda. In the six years since Sharpeville, the South African regime had introduced a torrent of 'security' legislation to match its segregation laws. President Verwoerd claimed his government was bound by its electoral mandate to resist racial integration, and that included letting Maori All Blacks play in South Africa. New Zealand's rugby administrators held to their old line, with Rugby Union president Tom Pearce arguing that, 'We have a duty to the Maoris, but also a duty to the game of rugby.' But this was becoming an increasingly isolated view. The Federation of Labour threatened to close hotels and public transport for any racially selected team. Newspaper editorials were uniformly against a racially selected All Black team, and Prime Minister Keith Holyoake broke the tradition of bland political neutrality, by stating that New Zealand could not be 'fully and truly represented by a team chosen on racial lines'.

> So instead of actually just writing and telling the South African Board, the Council decided that Tom Morrison, who was chairman at the time, and myself, should go through South Africa on our way to the International Board meeting in England. And we met the South African board at the Skyline Hotel in Johannesburg and told them that we wouldn't be coming. And that was that!
>
> *former Rugby Union chairman Ces Blazey*

The question of Maori players going to South Africa was finally settled by the assassination of Hendrik Verwoerd. His successor, Johannes Vorster, said that an All Black tour could include Maori — with the reported caveat that there not be too many, and they not be too black. The New Zealand Rugby Union hoped that the supposed breakthrough of having Maori players labelled 'honorary whites' would take the heat out of tour protests. But by this time the issue had grown beyond the domestic boundaries, to participation in an international movement to isolate South Africa entirely. The departure of the 1970 All Blacks was accompanied by massive protests and the first real confrontation between police and demonstrators, with 46 arrests made. And rugby's ranks were broken

. . . rugby's ranks were broken . . .

Four men to make history — Buff Milner, Blair Furlong, Sid Going and Bryan Williams, 1970.
Evening Post

when former All Black forward Ken Gray joined the opposition to the tour.

Nonetheless, four young men made history when they landed in Johannesburg to be welcomed by a crowd of 3000 rugby-mad South Africans. Sid Going, Blair Furlong and Henare 'Buff' Milner were all part-Maori, and with them was a brilliant 19-year-old Samoan winger who would become the star of the series, Bryan Williams.

It was God's will, without a doubt, that he should play this rugby.

> I must confess that when the plane touched down at Johannesburg airport I had this terrible panic come over me about what lay in store going to South Africa for the first time. And I really wanted that plane to turn right around and head back to New Zealand.
>
> *former All Black Bryan Williams*

> He played the best rugby I've ever seen anyone play on a rugby field. He was magnificent, and he was just God to the coloureds and blacks. And there lies a story too, because the whites didn't really like it. Here was the first black ever to play for New Zealand in South Africa and he played marvellous rugby. It was God's will, without a doubt, that he should play this rugby. And they were really a bit upset.
>
> *former All Black Grahame Thorne*

RUGBY VERSUS THE REST

Between the 1970 tour and the invitation for a return series in New Zealand in 1973, South Africa's place as a pariah nation was being fixed. A Springbok tour of Australia in 1971 had seen unprecedented civil unrest, with Queensland even declaring a state of emergency, and the Springbok team forced to travel in secret. In New Zealand, CARE and Halt All Racist Tours (HART) had proclaimed their intention to disrupt all sports events that included South Africans, and student protest leaders had begun calling for direct action at demonstrations.

New Zealand anti-apartheid organisations were also being recognised and offered support by the United Nations Special Committee on Apartheid. But although opposition to the proposed tour was now broad, it was not unanimous. Already, the lines that would crack in 1981 were showing up in all kinds of organisations. The Catholic hierarchy supported a tour in 1970, but the Catholic press strongly opposed it. The Anglican church was similarly split between anti-tour clergy and pro-tour lay representatives at their General Synod, and trade unionists, students and the general public were divided.

Politically, the tour issue was one of the main points of difference between the National Government and the Labour Opposition. The intensity of the debate

93

Prime Minister Norman Kirk, whose decision to force the cancellation of the 1973 Springbok tour contributed to his government's severe electoral problems.
John Selkirk

reflected a general erosion of the broad conservative consensus that had ruled in New Zealand since the 50s, and which had seen National in office for 20 of the last 23 years. Decades of prosperity and security were giving way to instability, both economic and social. When Norman Kirk's Labour Party won the landslide election in 1972, it marked an historical turning point for New Zealand. Rugby, of course, would play its part.

> When Norman Kirk won in 1972 we thought a new golden age was going to dawn. I remember it was a wonderful summer, it went on forever. I went on holiday around the South Island, and it stayed light until 10 o'clock at night. And I thought it had something to do with the Labour Government actually.
>
> *Warwick Roger*

Many things conspired to upset the high expectations of the Kirk administration. The liberal social agenda — recognising Communist China, withdrawal of troops from Vietnam, protests against French nuclear testing in the Pacific — was overshadowed by the bad news: the oil shocks, inflation, the collapse of wool prices. The proposed Springbok tour of 1973 was just another political grenade waiting to go off. Kirk had glossed over the issue during the election campaign,

. . . just another political grenade waiting to go off.

94

but promised not to interfere with arrangements already made. He reversed that pledge, pointing to police estimates of the cost and scale of widespread protest, and the effect on New Zealand's international reputation, particularly the consequences for the 1974 Commonwealth Games to be held in Christchurch. When it became clear the Rugby Union would not withdraw the invitation, Kirk threatened them with cancellation. Officially (and begrudgingly), the tour was deferred. But it was like drawing a line between two New Zealands — one that believed that sport and politics shouldn't be mixed, and one that did.

. . . it was like drawing a line between two New Zealands . . .

> I think Kirk would have been forgiven for a lot of the changes, even by people who weren't completely comfortable with the direction in which he was taking the country. But he did this other thing. He cancelled the rugby. And yes, it mattered in heartland New Zealand. At the moment he did that, he lost a whole raft of provincial Labour seats that they would not get back.
>
> *Ian Fraser*

> I think it was the beginning of the split. People began to talk about 'trendies' and 'wankers' and so on. And I think I began to understand quite clearly about then that I was a trendy and a wanker.
>
> *Warwick Roger*

Rugby may have been a catalyst for such a split, but it was also feeling the influences of social change itself. The new generation of players had been born after the war, raised during the 60s when television and air travel opened up the world to New Zealand, and New Zealand to the world. The short-back-and-sides stereotype was no longer the only man on the paddock.

> I remember a fellow called Bob Burgess who was a very good first five-eighth, and made the All Blacks in the early 70s. He had long hair down to his shoulders and a moustache. This was unknown – that a rugby player, and particularly an All Black, could actually look like his peers and contemporaries.
>
> *Warwick Roger*

> I remember having quite long hair in 1970 when I first started getting into the so-called big time. And there were newspaper editorials suggesting that I not be selected for teams until I got my hair cut.
>
> *writer Greg McGee*

In the wake of Kirk's untimely death in 1974, short-haired rugby would find its new champion. Robert Muldoon led the rejuvenated National Party into the 1975 election with the cancelled rugby tour as ammunition. At rallies up and

Robert Muldoon (pictured in 1981) rode to power on an election pledge to allow sporting contact with South Africa.
NZ Herald

down the country he played on nostalgia for past Springbok tours, and the commitment that future tours would not be stopped. 'We will play sport with all the world' was the campaign banner; unsubtle code for 'We'll let the Springboks in'.

Muldoon's victory was almost exactly simultaneous with a landmark call at the United Nations to boycott sports teams selected on the basis of race. New Zealand began to move steadily in the opposite direction to the rest of the world, something pointed out by Abraham Ordia, president of the Supreme Council for Sport in Africa, when he visited in 1976. Ordia explained the consequences if the proposed All Black tour of South Africa went ahead that year. African nations would boycott any sporting event where New Zealand participated. Muldoon's response was characteristically dismissive: 'He is not a diplomat or a member of a government,' he said on refusing to meet Ordia. 'He is some kind of sports administrator.' If New Zealand was turning a deaf ear, it would be made to listen when 21 African nations walked out of the Montreal Olympics. New Zealand rugby was now at the centre of an unprecedented crisis in the modern Olympic Games. The world's largest sporting festival had been damaged by a Rugby Union decision made 'in the best interests of rugby'.

> We came into the Olympic village about ten days before the opening, and I think we knew that there was the possibility of a boycott. We would often dine with some of the Kenyan and other African runners. We had a very good relationship. But as it progressed the tension started to grow. We saw less and less of them.
> As it started to unfold I think we realised how hopeless the situation was. That we were just pawns and we didn't really have a say in this. That was very frustrating. I think the anger started to come then at the Rugby Union because of their stand, and what I would call their arrogance.
>
> *athlete Rod Dixon*

The 1976 Games had held the promise of a classic athletics clash between the two best 1500-metre runners in the world, New Zealand's John Walker and Tanzanian Filbert Bayi. When Tanzania joined the boycott, it was all over. The

New Zealand athletes may have cursed rugby, but they shared one thing in common with the other sport — the bureaucratic presence of Cecil Albert Blazey, who was not only on the executive of the Rugby Union, but was also chairman of the New Zealand Amateur Athletics Association. Blazey has strenuously denied any conflict of interest, and regarded his twin roles as completely separate, 'like pulling down a blind on one, and letting another one up'. But this was cold comfort to the runners and other athletes for whom an Olympic Games is literally the chance of a lifetime to compete at that level. The effect of the walkout, when it happened, was devastating.

> I remember a team member telling me that he got in a lift in one of the apartment blocks that they were in, and he got one floor and the doors opened and there was a whole bundle of Kenyans with their bags going home. And he thought, whoa, I'm in for it here. And they all recognised him immediately with his New Zealand uniform, and they said, oh, we're going home, it's terrible. And some of them started crying and they all shook his hand and wished him well at the Games. The emotion that was around wasn't what you'd expect. It was anger, but it was sympathy for the whole situation.
>
> *athlete and coach John Davies*

> My mind was completely changed by the events over those three months in 1976. I left for the trip to the Olympics and the All Blacks tour as a rugby clunker. I had the mentaiity that the most important thing was that John Walker beat Filbert Bayi in the 1500 metres, and that we stuff the Springboks in the test series. But with the boycott in Montreal, and then going to South Africa and seeing apartheid, and how badly black people were treated, my whole opinion of the question was turned around.
>
> *television commentator Keith Quinn*

By this time, New Zealand's own myths of racial harmony were being put to the test. In 1975 a Maori land march led by Whina Cooper took the slogan 'not one more acre of Maori land' to 75 marae *en route* from Te Hapua in the north to Wellington. Two years later, Joe Hawke led a 506-day occupation of Auckland's Bastion Point by the Orakei Maori Action Committee, in protest at the alienation of Ngati Whatua land by the Crown. Maybe, some began to think, the great melting pot of rugby was not the racially indifferent arena that New Zealanders had come to assume it was.

> It might sound harsh but reality usually is, when you say that, yes, you were accepted while you were playing and you were a good rugby player. You

. . . New Zealand's own myths of racial harmony were being put to the test.

would be accepted to have a few beers after the game and maybe even given a job to keep you in the local team. But after the game was over and the ability of that player waned, then that conviviality changed somewhat.

Jim Perry

It developed a myth, really a lie, that integration did in fact occur on the sports field. That we were all one, that we all worked together. And perhaps to some extent in a team, that did happen. But I found that whenever someone wanted to rile me on the football field, and I had a very short temper I'm told, they would always talk to me and abuse me in racist and offensive terms. So I was always a black bastard and that would be one of the most kind terms that I would have directed at me.

Syd Jackson

South Africa's racial conflict had escalated. Flushed with confidence after independence victories in bordering Angola and Mozambique, younger South African blacks took a more defiant and assertive stance than their parents. On 16 March 1976, black students marching in protest against the enforced teaching of the Afrikaans language were shot at by police in Soweto, and 13-year-old Hector Peterson was killed. The township erupted. In one week, 176 people were killed as the violence spread to other communities. The government responded with ever more repressive strategies. Near the end of 1977, Steve Biko, the inspirational black consciousness leader, had been beaten and shackled naked in a police van, later to die of brain damage from blows to the head.

South African President Johannes Vorster projects a publicly calm face as his country descends further into civil unrest during another All Black tour.
NZ Herald

Like Sharpeville before, the Soweto uprising coincided eerily with an All Black tour. Throughout the series, the All Blacks and their supporters from home were dogged by protests and disturbances that belied President Vorster's claim that 'there is no crisis'. After the débâcle at Montreal, it was becoming increasingly difficult to pretend that rugby with South Africa could remain above it all.

Muldoon appeared to acknowledge as much when he supported and signed the Gleneagles Agreement in 1977, which said that Commonwealth governments should take every possible step to discourage sporting contact with South Africa. If this meant that New Zealand was now walking in step with international policy, it also meant that Muldoon was effectively reversing his election vow that rugby tours would be free of interference. In light of what was about to happen, it is clear that he was playing a political game to appease both his national constituency and international opinion.

There was no diversity of views which could be authentic and allowable.

> It was a game all the time of doing enough to placate the rest of the world but doing it grudgingly, and constantly winking at heartland New Zealand, saying, well, we know what this really means, don't we?
>
> *Ian Fraser*

It was a dangerous game. There were several heartlands now, and winking at one often meant snubbing another. Rugby was on the verge of becoming the receptacle of a nation's racial, social and generational problems. It was far more than a game could take.

> There was a feeling that the Muldoon government was a divide-and-rule one. That it represented not charity any more, but various forms of hatred. That it said, it's them, it's him — that is why you feel disaffected, this is why you feel unhappy. That it categorised people. There was Rob's Mob and that you belonged to that or you weren't really a Kiwi. There was no diversity of views which could be authentic and allowable. That you were beyond the pale, or you were within.
>
> *Tony Reid*

THE LAST TOUR

During the Springbok tour of 1981, Canterbury University sociologist Geoff Fougere sat down to write to a friend in the United States to explain what was happening in New Zealand. Part way through the letter he realised that none of it was comprehensible to an American.

> Unless you'd grown up here, then the events that I was relating just simply didn't make sense. It was the assumptions that I was bringing to it as a New Zealander, my implicit understanding of how rugby fitted into this country, that provided the frame in which you can make sense of these events. What was the role that rugby played in our country? Why was it so important? Why was it an area which had led people to be so polarised, so divided?
>
> *Geoff Fougere*

The record shows that the Springboks came to New Zealand, played fourteen provincial matches, with one cancelled, and three tests against the All Blacks. As usual it was hard-fought rugby, uncompromising, played for keeps. The record

Long after the tour, the answer to the question 'Why?' is still elusive.

also shows that New Zealand won the test series two-one. The rugby crown was back.

But unlike other test series in rugby history, there is no cherished collective memory of the games. Nobody really remembers the rugby. Everybody remembers what rugby did to New Zealand. Long after the tour, the answer to the question 'Why?' is still elusive.

> The funny thing about it is that you would have thought this far on, we were really living in a completely different culture and you should be able to look back and say what those forces were. It should be reasonably clear by now, but I don't think it is.
>
> *Tony Reid*

As in 1956 and 1965 the Springbok team was officially welcomed at Poho-o-Rawiri marae in Gisborne. Long deliberation had taken place within the local iwi, who were well aware that there would be dissenters to this traditional show of hospitality. To try to defuse some tensions, marae elders invited protesters to the marae to have their say before the welcome. Police were kept away, and Maori wardens and Mongrel Mob members employed to patrol the perimeter

Over 60 years of rugby with South Africa culminates in street warfare in New Zealand, final test, Auckland, 1981. But for their ideas, they are indistinguishable.
John Selkirk

and car park. The local chapter of HART pledged not to disrupt the powhiri. When the Springboks arrived, however, there was a small crowd that had been locked out of the marae. The rugby players jogged, frozen-faced, through the protesters to the entrance. The jeers were as much for those inside as for the team itself: accusations of betrayal, of treachery, invocations of ancestors, war heroes, the Maori Battalion. Maori versus Maori. Inside, Graham Latimer would tell the South Africans that this was their last welcome on a marae unless their government changed its racial policy. It was too little, too late, for those outside.

The cracks spread into every corner of New Zealand society. Hardly a New Zealander could say that everyone they knew agreed with them about the Springbok tour.

> As a former All Black and a person who believed in what these people were saying, I felt it was appropriate that I should get up and say that I did not support the tour. It certainly caused some problems with the people that I knew well who were fanatics about the game and could not see an All Black doing those sorts of things or saying them.
>
> *John Graham*

> Most of my friends were in the front line every Wednesday and Saturday and I was part of the government that was providing funds for them to be beaten with batons and hit on the head and mauled and all kinds of other things. So it was very, very tough.
>
> *former National member of parliament Marilyn Waring*

For at least one New Zealander, the '81 tour represented a personal crisis as well as a national one. Cartoonist Murray Ball, creator of the classic slice of rural life, *Footrot Flats*, had a unique connection with South Africa and rugby. Son of the 1930s All Black Nelson Ball, Murray had emigrated with the family to South Africa in 1948 (a year before Daniel Malan led the National Party to victory and began the institutionalisation of apartheid). As a ten-year-old schoolboy he witnessed the humiliating defeat of the 1949 All Blacks, and was tormented by his Afrikaaner school mates. An excellent rugby player himself, he always wanted to emulate his father's achievements. After returning to New Zealand, he made the New Zealand Juniors in 1959, was an All Black triallist the same year, and represented Manawatu and Wellington. The 'No Maoris — No Tour' movement had largely passed him by, but by 1981 he was convinced that South Africa was a sick society. He withdrew the cartoon strip's famous 'Dog' as the All Blacks' unofficial mascot, and joined the first protest march in Gisborne.

The cracks spread into every corner of New Zealand society.

101

Auckland, 1981.
Marti Friedlander

Personally my most vivid memory was the total destruction of my family. I had a lot of relations in South Africa. My father had remarried a South African woman, a very nice woman, and we were very close as a family. My sister had married a South African and I've got South African nephews and nieces. My family is split in half. Half of them are in South Africa, a lot of them are New Zealanders in South Africa, but some of them are South Africans in South Africa. My brother and I were standing on one side of the fence against the tour and my father, who we loved and admired, was on the other side saying we were making absolute fools of ourselves. It took us years and years to recover from that rift. Not so much with Dad, but with the rest of the family. There's always that tension and it's only in comparatively recent times that we can even talk about that period.

Murray Ball

The National Government was aware that a tour would probably provoke civil unrest, and that police resources might be stretched. Foreign Affairs Minister Brian Talboys even wrote to the Rugby Union when it met to formally issue the invitation, expressing his 'deep concern' that such a tour might take place. But whereas the police had told Kirk that a tour might engender the 'greatest eruption of violence this country has ever known', the official view was that any disruption could be handled.

Initially the Government appeared to be applying pressure on the Union to reconsider. Muldoon expressed his opposition to the tour. But the basic policy remained; no political interference in the rights of sporting bodies to make their own decisions. On 6 July 1981 Muldoon declared that, 'The Government will not order the Rugby Union to abandon the tour.' By this late stage, of course, to have ordered the Rugby Union to back down would have been politically damaging — except that such a move could have been made much earlier when the rugby community's expectations weren't as high. The conclusion that many reached was that Muldoon had opted to allow the tour for electoral gain: 1981 was also an election year.

There were a lot of mixed-up agendas within that protest movement and one of the strongest was an anti-Muldoon sentiment. Remember by '81 Muldoon had virtually alienated every sector of society and there were a lot of people out there who recognised that tour as Muldoon's cynical attempt to appeal to the rural marginals, and were protesting against that.

Greg McGee

Muldoon dealt superbly with the tours of '76 and '81, exactly according to his political creed. His political creed was very simple — a majority is 51, a minority is 49 and he unerringly went for the majority. And he also had another simple philosophy which was that if you make the minority mad as hell you can get bigger kudos out of it. So that's what he did.

David Lange

I think that the Rugby Union behaved appallingly because they should have cancelled the tour anyway, and no group of people who have any con-sciousness about international human rights and who chose to play sport beyond national boundaries, should have to wait for a government to wave its big finger about whether or not it participates.

Marilyn Waring

You can be very unfair to the Rugby Union . . . you see the difficulty with the Rugby Union is it's not there to represent the interests of the country. The Rugby Union people are elected to represent the interests of those people for whom rugby is a devoted sport or religion.

David Lange

I think that the Rugby Union behaved appallingly . . .

CONFRONTING OURSELVES

In 1956, Hamilton had been the scene of extraordinary celebration when the Springboks came to town — crowds, a parade, delight in hosting these exotic visitors. Quarter of a century on, the Waikato game was cancelled when demon-strators invaded the pitch. Television sports cameras, there to record a game of rugby, instead beamed a protest drama live to New Zealand's living rooms. In South Africa it was still night, and the white rugby community had dragged itself from bed to watch the first live televised Springbok game from overseas since the country had been networked five years earlier.

When the protesters broke through onto the middle of that field, you had a kind of obscene geometry. You had forces lined up, you had the crowd around chanting 'kill, kill, kill'. You had then the riot police for the first time seen in New Zealand and their visors and long truncheons and so on all around the field . . .

Tony Reid

You had forces lined up, you had the crowd around chanting 'kill, kill, kill'.

I was outside and I remember thinking how innocent we were as protesters because when the game was called off this huge cheer went up and everyone started dancing around and Tim Shadbolt had a loud-hailer and he was saying, 'We've done it, we've done it, the tour is off, the tour is off.' And all I could think of was those fans who were going to come out shortly. And I remember going to Tim and telling him, 'They're going to come out, get us out of here, get us out of here.'

Greg McGee

I was arrested and was placed in the paddy wagon and taken to the cells courtesy of the police. Just as we were coming out of the park on to the street there was this young Maori guy attacked the side of the van, was beating on it with his fists and screaming out that we'd ruined the best fuckin' day of his life, and demanding that the police let us out. So we were encouraged to reply in kind. But that was how deeply he felt that day.

Syd Jackson

The crowd went berserk. It was like some big . . . poisonous lump of phlegm being released in the national throat. There was this incredible feeling of release. People went berserk . . . People drove in to hit the protesters. They brought their children with them. They hit everyone in sight. I saw them hitting each other, the release was such. It was an extraordinary thing to watch and I think a lot of it was kind of a blind rage. We were meant to be one people, we were meant to like rugby, and we weren't anymore. These people in the middle were aliens and the people in the middle thought the people around them were kind of fascist thugs.

Tony Reid

I think we saw the sporting face of Rob's Mob at Rugby Park . . . when the protesters came on to the centre of the field. I wasn't there but I have close friends who were there and they came back telling these incredible war stories. And they had looked into the face of Rob's Mob and had seen the hatred in the eyes of Rob's Mob and they were shit-scared.

Warwick Roger

The crowd was angry and bewildered. There were various things happening. There were these people who were mainly city people who had come down. Once upon a time city and country were the same. Once upon a time you weren't a Kiwi unless you stood by rugby.

Tony Reid

Inside caucus from week to week, whether it was the provision of more barbed wire, the cancellation of police leave, calling out the army, whatever it was, everything, all government resources, were mobilised to make sure that apartheid sport was played. And the only game that was cancelled was extraordinarily cynically cancelled in a Labour-held marginal. And there were definitely rugby grounds that were far more difficult to secure, as they

People went berserk . . . People drove in to hit the protesters.

used to say, but just more resources were given to National-held marginals to secure the ground.

Marilyn Waring

The tour marched on: New Plymouth, Wellington, Palmerston North, Wanganui, Invercargill, Dunedin, Christchurch, Greymouth, Nelson, Napier, Wellington again, Rotorua. New Zealanders became accustomed to the sights — helmets, long batons, loud-hailers, aeroplanes, flour bombs, blood. The third and last test was played in Auckland, and whatever the protests had been about in the beginning, they had now become street warfare.

And really what I remember wasn't just the violence, it was the hatred that was on both sides . . . It was like a force-field, it was something palpable. And the Patu Squad versus the Red Squad — I mean, look at the words, you know? Smashing hell out of each other and then being carted off in the same ambulances.

What it was about at that stage I don't know. It was about apartheid, it was about a whole lot of things. There were forces unleashed which I don't think were directly to do with anything.

Tony Reid

Even diehard tour supporters baulked at the notion of rugby played behind barbed wire, Christchurch, 1981.
John Selkirk

So what was it about? Apartheid, racism, Muldoon, rugby, South Africa, New Zealand? Had it been coming since the New Zealand Services All Blacks let South Africans tell them to leave Ranji Wilson on the ship in 1919? Or was it the product of a more immediate history, the logical conclusion of Muldoon's divisive style of leadership? Did it teach New Zealand anything lasting, or did it merely confuse?

I didn't think the protest was just about South Africa. I thought it was an internal squabble and it was frustration, incredible frustration that the country just wasn't shifting. We were dominated by a very grey regime, a very grey lifestyle and the game filtered into every area of life and perhaps had too much influence. It was dictating our foreign policy. That was unacceptable to everybody, probably myself as well.

Lloyd Jones

For those who were sincere, they were making a statement which was international and had got outside the concept that rugby is all-consuming in this country and is sacred and should not be touched. And in that sense it was a very important part of the growing up of the nation in terms of its approach to sport. A most significant change.

John Graham

I do think it was just an enormous mobilisation of New Zealand people across the widest possible margin who were really tired of the tyranny of white man's culture, exemplified by rugby and all that it meant.

Marilyn Waring

. . . it was about two competing views of patriotic pride . . .

It seems to me looking back on it that as much as anything it was about two competing views of patriotic pride and both had a lot to do with the Muldoon government.

Tony Reid

The anti-tour people and the pro-tour people were talking the same language — either you're with us or against us. One for all, all for one. And that was a recipe for disaster and it was anti-intellectual. There was no scope for having a slightly different shade of opinion.

Lloyd Jones

One of the funny things that happened after the tour was, at first you might have thought it was simply exhaustion, but was almost a conspiracy of silence. Nobody would talk about it. It was over, nobody got a second wind. It was not a discussable thing.

Tony Reid

28.
A sight to shock our forebears, for whom the thought of 'muscular maidens' playing physical games would have been little short of scandalous. Now the clubs run créches to allow mothers to play. Here the Wellington Rugby Union's women's provincial team is playing Manawatu at the Petone Recreation Ground.

29.
The Wellington women's team pays the price for victory in injuries, just like the blokes. It's a far cry from the post-war years when women's rugby was a novelty curtain-raiser, and physical contact was avoided.

30.
Not the biggest crowds, of course, but these days it is often the little boys on the sideline watching mum play, not the other way around.

31.
*And as New
Zealanders have
always been noted for
doing, women play
rugby just like their
male counterparts —
hard, and to win.*

32.
*At the Eden Club in Auckland's
Sandringham in 1995, the
annual prizegiving marks the
end of yet another season.*

33.
Little boys and their mothers. Most improved players, best sports, highest scorers, best team spirit . . . something for every-one at Auckland's Eden Club.

34.
The nursery grade team photo, memento of a time that will inevitably become a distant memory, another rugby milestone on life's road. Eden Club, 1995.

35.
The early glimmerings of the rewards that rugby can bring — and the team photos that might yet be.

Rugby had been New Zealand's way of celebrating itself, as Geoff Fougere puts it. It was one part of life where the country could face the world and come first, not cringe or explain away. It was common cause, identity and entertainment rolled together. But 1981 turned all that on its head. Now rugby was symbolic of difference, of intolerance, of our place in the world in a negative sense. New Zealand had changed immeasurably — Maori-Pakeha relations, trading partners, the role of women — and rugby hadn't kept up. Large sections of society openly scorned the game and its associated aggressive male culture. The next decade and a half would see whether rugby could find a new place in the country.

Now rugby was symbolic of difference, of intolerance, of our place in the world in a negative sense.

FULL CIRCLE

Rugby's fall from grace was compounded in the early 1980s by several coincidental events. No sooner had the Springbok tour of 1981 done its damage, than soccer — the perennial poor cousin in the family of New Zealand sport — rocketed to unprecedented popularity when the All Whites qualified for the final round of the World Cup. Rugby was also getting a bad press due to a spate of serious spinal injuries in schoolboy games, apparent proof of the game's rash brutality. Combine these with the fact that schoolteaching — particularly at primary level — had seen a big increase in the number of women teachers, and a move away from rugby at the nursery grades seemed almost inevitable. Middle-class teachers and parents who had marched against the tour could maintain their protest, and their children needed less coaxing than before to accept another sporting code. If there was a low point for rugby, to match the peak of collective fixation witnessed in 1956, then this was it.

The seismic shockwaves from 1981 were felt at the general election in 1984. Three years earlier Muldoon had held power in the wake of the proxy civil war, but it was a last gasp. The second great post-war era of conservative government staggered on, until Muldoon, uncharacteristically misreading the electorate, called a snap poll and brought down a Labour landslide on his administration.

And in 1984 you had this remarkable thing. Not just the fact that we had a revolution in terms of the market being allowed to rule, and all this deregulation. But I see it in generational terms. That the flame was handed over, not to the next generation as you might have expected, but to the generation beyond that. And I don't think that had happened before in the history of New Zealand politics, and I don't think it can be underestimated.

Ian Fraser

David Lange's government set sail under a flag of consensus, and, true to form, rugby was one of the first tests of its idealism. Another All Black tour of South Africa was on the international rugby calender, and the Union was showing every sign of going. Kirk had proved in 1973 that an inbound tour could be halted, and Holyoake had earlier shown that the Union could be persuaded to call off an outbound tour. New to the game, Lange's only option, short of banning the team from leaving the country, was to persuade the Union to abandon the tour.

> And being reduced to moral suasion in the Rugby Union that I knew was being reduced to impotence. Because moral suasion had no effect on people for whom rugby was transcendental.
>
> *David Lange*

Ironically, the Rugby Union's traditional justification for playing with South Africa — that its job was simply to foster and develop the game — was now its Achilles heel. Two rugby-playing lawyers, Phil Recordon and Paddy Finnigan, took the Union to court on the grounds that, contrary to the Union's own charter, a South African tour would not be in the best interests of rugby. In fact, the Rugby Union council was already split over this very issue (although a clear majority eventually voted for the tour), and two provincial unions, Auckland and North Harbour, also voted against a tour. The legal challenge was rejected in the High Court on a technicality (the lawyers' club memberships did not entitle them to a cause of action against the Union), but this was overturned by the Court of Appeal. Going back to the High Court, Recordon and Finnigan obtained an injunction that effectively blocked the tour before the case could be heard in full.

> I don't know that I've ever experienced in politics or in law or in any part of my life such an exquisite relief.
>
> *David Lange*

In an echo of the social breakdown that rugby had caused in 1981, the game's own structure now began to disintegrate. The secretly organised rebel tour by All Black players calling themselves, fittingly, the Cavaliers, showed that the attractions of playing South Africa were stronger even than loyalty to their own Union. All Black great Colin Meads, co-manager of the Cavaliers, said the tour would 'open a door that should never have been closed'. In fact, it had exactly the opposite effect. The New Zealand Union was outraged by Danie Craven's

. . . the game's own structure now began to disintegrate.

conspiracy — the Cavaliers enjoyed the full itinerary and support of an official tour — and Ces Blazey told him as much at a rugby congress in England. In typically genteel style, he announced to Craven that it was 'unacceptable'. Craven's appropriately cavalier response was to ask a colleague what 'unacceptable' meant. The upshot was a paradox: the rugby establishment, at times South Africa's last and loneliest ally, was now on side with its old foe, the anti-tour movement.

> Their constant argument was that they were there to administer rugby and not to enforce the foreign policy of the New Zealand government. And the more people argued against what they were doing, I think, the more entrenched their views became. So in a sense, the Cavaliers were good because by 1985 they were doing the wrong thing and all of a sudden the Rugby Union was seen to be doing the right thing, and it was able to move away from that entrenched position.
>
> *Ron Palenski*

In the end, New Zealand rugby weathered the storms of the 1980s. It remade itself in time to win the inaugural World Cup in 1987; honed, polished, more PR-conscious. Led by would-be politician David Kirk, the world-champion All

Auckland, 1981. Three years after a winter of scenes like this, the Rugby Union prepared to play South Africa yet again.
Estate of Robin Morrison

Blacks seemed to suit the glamour of the deregulated frontier economy created by the Labour Government. South Africa was now off the itinerary — but not for long. The year after the All Blacks won the World Cup, more blacks than whites graduated from South African universities. The white regime could read the signs — apartheid had never been a workable policy in practice — and was soon engaged in secret negotiations for the transition of power and majority rule.

Neither George Nepia nor any of the Maori players touched by the racism of another country could have guessed that their lives would have a final, posthumous chapter. And yet, in the majestic sporting theatre of Ellis Park in Johannesburg, before the final of the 1995 Rugby World Cup, their story finally ended. Seventy-five years after Ranji Wilson stayed on the ship in Cape Town harbour, a black president of South Africa put on a Springbok jersey — once a badge of his oppressor — and greeted the world's newest rugby superstar, a brown giant in an All Black jersey named Jonah Lomu.

> Watching the World Cup and seeing Nelson Mandela embrace the game, I thought how ironic. But this was a happy ending, and for the first time I felt the chapter was closed. And poetically the leader of the anti-apartheid movement and the fight for black equality in Africa, Nelson Mandela, was closing it for New Zealand rugby. Because he saw in rugby something that we ourselves have found over the past hundred years — that here is a game that can be more than a game.
>
> *Ian Cross*

POSTSCRIPT: Later in 1995, Nelson Mandela visited New Zealand for the Commonwealth Heads of Government Meeting in Auckland. Staying on for several engagements, including a church service for veterans of the local anti-apartheid movement, he drew admiring crowds wherever he went. His tour coincided with another royal visit, but Mandela upstaged Queen Elizabeth II in the affections of New Zealanders. Politicians who had openly criticised David Lange's ground-breaking prime ministerial tour of Southern Africa in 1985, during which he met representatives of the African National Congress, now queued to bask in the President's reflected glory. Reporters spoke of Mandela's 'almost spiritual' presence. Little girls wept when he greeted them. The man who had spent a third of his life behind bars, while New Zealand played four official and one unofficial rugby series with his jailers, seemed to elicit an unspoken acknowledgement that the protests had been right. Mandela's own 'long walk to freedom' is an inspiring journey, and New Zealanders were glad to have been a part of it.

. . . an unspoken acknowledgement that the protests had been right.

Part 4

THE MORE THINGS CHANGE ...

Saturday — it's the name of our game . . .
Lotto advertisement

The shapes and sounds of Saturday have changed. When rugby ruled the land, the suburbs rang to the sound of boots on a leather ball and cheers from the sidelines. In the 1990s, the ring is from cash registers on the busiest shopping day of the week. Saturday is no longer a day of leisure for many New Zealanders. It's another work day in the competitive market economy that has replaced the old certainties of the welfare state. Saturday was enshrined gradually as the nation's day of freedom and fun, from William Pember Reeves' labour legislation in the 1890s to the forty-hour week becoming standard after the Second World War. A decade of deregulation in the 1980s and 90s undid those cultural fastenings, and set rugby loose to compete for the leisure dollar. The national game has become an international money-spinner and its top players can become millionaires.

Stars of the modern game might employ lawyers to negotiate their contracts, carry cell-phones and drive expensive cars, but the small-time world from which they all emerged is remarkably recognisable. The Eden club in Auckland sits in the middle of a demographic snapshot of the city — Pakeha, Pacific Island and Maori families with a rising Asian population, in a suburban setting of modest rental houses and an increasing number of renovated villas and bungalows. In the chilly twilight of a mid-week practice run, rugby looks as familiar as ever. Outside the corner dairies, however, the kids are playing endless video games. They wear Auckland Warriors jerseys and backwards baseball caps. They're conscious of the labels on their jeans and their sweatshirts, and they certainly don't all make the pilgrimage to Eden Park, just down Sandringham Road, if there's a big game on.

The whole rhythm of the week has changed. It's not the pivotal day of the week any more. The big sports event is no longer just played on Saturday.

We have league on Friday nights. We're just as likely to watch a rugby test on a Sunday now, or perhaps late on a Saturday as it's being televised from Sydney . . . Television is the organising influence, not the suburb.

Lloyd Jones

Everything has changed, but nothing has changed. Inside the Eden clubhouse on prize-giving night, time slips away. As the trophies and cups and plaques are handed out — most-improved player, most tries scored, best sportsmanship — the rapt attention and eagerness is the same as it has always been. The end of another rugby season, a little recognition, something to aspire to next year. Mates. For the grown-ups, there's a bar where they serve jugs of Lion beer, some stand-up tables with holes in the middle for ashtrays, and a kitchen doing pies and chips and fried chicken. The money that goes across the counter goes back into the club. The people pulling the pints and serving the meals are volunteers, just like the coaches and the organisers. Rugby became a professional sport in 1995, but down at the local club it's strictly amateur hour. Same as it ever was.

. . . down at the local club it's strictly amateur hour. Same as it ever was.

My first memory of a rugby club goes back to when I was five years of age. I was one of those youngsters who had a father who continued playing rugby until he was in his 40s. So as a consequence I overlapped in my playing career with my dad. I played in the half-time breaks at senior matches when Dad was playing for United on Rugby Park, Greymouth. And I became part of a little midget team which every month was taken by a coach to a local hall where we were shown movies for the evening — Groucho Marx, Bud Abbott and Lou Costello — and we were given ice-creams. And that seemed to me as a five-year-old to be what rugby clubs were about. They were about Bud Abbott and Lou Costello and having an ice-cream and having a good time. I think we hardly ever won any games and I don't think the coach knew a great deal about rugby to be honest! But he knew a lot about kids.

Len Richardson

One of the stars at the Eden club is Brett Kamutoa, 13 years old and already progressing out of the everyday world of junior grades rugby into the serious business of representative competition. This year, he has been chosen for the West Auckland team in the northern North Island primary school rugby tournament, sponsored by the Champion Roller Mills company. For 75 years, 'the Roller Mills' has been the first stepping-stone of many talented players on their way to provincial or national representative status. It's their first taste of the dedication needed to succeed at the higher levels of sport, and for Brett it means watching his weight in a way that most kids his age never have to. Since the last rugby season he has shot up from 45 kilograms to nearly 54, threatening his eligibility to play in the restricted weight grade. His mother, Fetu, caught him sneaking a packet of chips one day, though Brett tried to pretend it belonged to a friend. 'I just feel like strangling him,' she jokes. But such are the privations of a boy on the road to rugby glory.

The Kamutoas are Niuean New Zealanders. Brett is the only boy among their four children, and the repository of his parents' sporting dreams. Fetu herself is a talented touch rugby player and has represented Niue overseas at this modern variant of the game. Dad Tony played league, and works nights unloading imported Japanese cars on the Auckland wharves. Their lives are busy with work and children, often too busy to fully appreciate how well Brett is doing at rugby. 'We don't realise he's playing really good football until somebody else tells us,' says Fetu. 'We're just running around so much, which is a bit hard.'

HARD TIMES

The decade between 1984 and 1995 was hard on a lot of people. Champion Roller Mills, sponsors of Brett Kamutoa's tournament, underwent its own restructuring in 1987, when the wheat-processing industry was completely deregulated. From having one customer — the Wheat Board — in 1986, the company has 650 individual customers. A marketing arm had to be established and new relationships forged with the users of the Roller Mills products. Staff numbers dropped from a pre-deregulation high of about 140 to 88 within two years and down to 59 in 1995. The remaining workers went on retraining courses to meet the demands of the newly competitive industry; Roller Mills is New Zealand industry in microcosm.

Effectively you've got people playing in different positions, you've got to use the entire team, you've got to make sure the people are compatible, that they're aware of what their internal customer does, so they can receive their passes correctly, and they can pass on the product that they're handling to the next stage in the process.
Champion Roller Mills managing director Ron Bates

. . . you've got to make sure the people are compatible . . .

The sponsorship of schoolboy rugby began in 1924, but the Northern Roller Milling Company had, in fact, sponsored rugby and rugby league as early as 1902. For most of its history the company's involvement was largely altruistic, with no appreciable commercial advantage accruing, and indeed no great

113

competition within the industry for market share. That too has changed, with a public relations firm now engaged to ensure that the company's main brand — Champion — is associated with the tournament. Paradoxically, one of the big selling points of the sponsorship is the company's venerable history and tradition, but part of that tradition is the tournament's popularly abbreviated title of 'the Roller Mills'. Change is never simple.

Down on the shop floor works Graham Gaskill, who started with the company in 1976, before the introduction of much of the mechanisation that made jobs redundant. Gaskill became the union delegate in the mid-80s, overcoming a distrust of unionism born of working on farms, and a dislike of the sharp demarcation lines of the old award system. The job losses, he says, were gradual, and the new environment is more efficient, with greater co-operation between staff and management. The old invisible line in the canteen between suits and overalls has disappeared. But Gaskill's association with the company goes back even further — although it wasn't until he arrived at Northern Roller Mills that he made the connection between his new employer and the schoolboy rugby grail he once strove for.

. . . you never, ever, wore shoes, otherwise you were called a sissy . . .

> I used to play rugby when I was at primary school in Pukekawa. And I can remember every Saturday morning I used to walk five kilometres, barefoot — you never, ever, wore shoes, otherwise you were called a sissy — on a metal road, and sometimes frost and ice, to catch a bus to go into Tuakau, and that's where our Saturday rugby was. Every Saturday morning we did that. And getting near the end of the season we had the trials for the Roller Mills team. I never made the team, but I got picked for the trials which was a great thrill . . . And it was sort of incredible to be playing, getting picked for the trials as a schoolkid and then ending up working for the same place.
> *silo man Graham Gaskill*

The impact of the economic direction pursued by the fourth Labour Government and its successor National Government is well documented. Labour Finance Minister Roger Douglas reversed a previous decade of regulation by Robert Muldoon (during which the Treasury had been largely ignored and had devoted a lot of time and energy to developing the alternative policies adopted by Labour). Import and export controls were torn down, the exchange rate floated and New Zealand's national economy opened to the vagaries of the 'international marketplace'. Foreign debt and unemployment both nearly quadrupled from 1984 to the early 1990s. Most New Zealanders experienced a constrained standard of living, and the country as a whole showed very slow and sometimes negative economic growth. Manufacturing was hardest hit by the flood of unrestricted cheap imports, and most jobs were lost in that sector. Similarly, no jobs were found to replace those made redundant by new technologies. Trade union power was severely curtailed by the National Government's Employment Contracts Act, but even this apparent assault on collectivism was justified by some as a move towards co-operative labour relations. 'My own view, based on first-hand experience, is that the Employment Contracts Act has created an opportunity to build a team approach to employee relations,' said rugby coach John Hart in Paul Thomas's biography, *Straight From the Hart*. Some called it market liberal-isation and some called it market totalitarianism, but the economic revolution of the 1980s and 90s was consistent with worldwide trends, made vogue by politicians like Ronald Reagan and Margaret Thatcher.

First to feel this global whirlwind in New Zealand were the farmers, who for years had enjoyed state protection and subsidisation of their products. With these gone, incomes fell and many farmers went to the wall. In central Hawke's Bay, one of the richest farming areas in New Zealand, the effects were no differ-ent. Fraser Kingston, a local historian, remembers his own father buying a new Chevrolet with the proceeds from three bales of wool. In the 1990s an equiva-lent purchase would require at least 100 bales. In the farming boom after the war and before Britain entered the EEC, Hawke's Bay farmers could afford to employ a man to do little more than kill the mutton for the dogs. Every farm had its own fencers. In the 1950s, 1200 ewes qualified as an economic unit; in the 1990s it takes more than twice that to turn a profit. A modern farmer manages three times the stock numbers he did in the 1960s without any increase in his purchasing power.

Economic deregulation meant the farms got leaner, poorer and more effi-cient. One of the most striking symptoms was the struggle faced by the small rugby clubs that had traditionally been centres of community activity and pride. With few men on the land, there were fewer on the rugby paddock. Long gone were the days of one farm being able to field a team of shepherds and labourers. The problem was compounded by the closing of the big meatworks, and by the removal of small-town post offices and hospitals as the knives of economic effi-ciency cut deeper. Where once the local farmers might have given a man a job if he played for the local rugby club, there was now an identifiable aversion to employing top players; with farms so financially fine-tuned there was no slack for workers taking time off for play or because of injury. But perhaps the most

With few men on the land, there were fewer on the rugby paddock.

vivid example of the new economy's influence was the way in which historical club rivalries were buried by rugby's need to survive.

The Waipawa River is more than just a geographical barrier between the towns of Waipawa and Waipukurau, it's the border between two fierce rugby communities. The annual match between the Waipawa United Rugby Football Club and Waipukurau High School Old Boys Club used to be called 'the battle of the bridge' (although old-timers will tell you that this was a bit of 'media beat-up'), and became something of a local jamboree day. Rivalry was always good-natured but intense, fed by club loyalties passed down through generations of players. But in the 1990s it became clear that neither club had the numbers to sustain itself, or to keep its talented players from straying to the richer clubs of Hastings and Napier. Amalgamation was the only logical solution, and in 1993 a new club, Central, was formed from the once great adversaries. While most involved could see the point, it was a difficult time.

> We had to get a change in mind-set, a change in thinking. It was slow because of a wonderful thing called club pride. There were a lot of people who could see the logic of it but who still said, I've been a Waipawa United or Waipukurau High School Old Boys stalwart and I don't want to see the identity of my club go. Some would call that parochialism. I call it real good pride.
> *former Waipukurau High School Old Boys chairman David Petersen*

After almost fifty years, it's a big part of your life.

> I think for anybody to say that they wouldn't feel that way, there's something wrong with them. After almost fifty years, it's a big part of your life. You almost feel as though you're losing your right arm . . .
> *Waipawa United Club member 1947–1993 Fraser Kingston*

Ironically, the man who finally brokered the amalgamation, John Berry, was himself a refugee from the restructuring of the global corporate jungle. As managing director of the local arm of a foreign corporation, he decided to jump ship when head office in the United States voted to amalgamate its New Zealand and Australian operations. After the sharemarket crash in 1987, land prices in the Hawke's Bay (where his mother came from) plummeted, allowing him to retreat from Auckland and buy a farm. A former player, he had served on the Counties Union and was soon asked to join the Central Hawke's Bay sub-union, and later to manage the formation of the Central Club. Despite the resistance of die-hard life members, he says, it has been a simple case of adapt or perish.

The very, very small rural communities have folded. Even though this is a small rural community in its own way, there were even smaller satellite communities. And they're the ones that have really suffered. The small country teams are disappearing, but there's always going to be a place for them. As long as you've got fifteen guys and they play rugby, I think that's where New Zealand will maintain its rugby roots.

John Berry

The small country teams are disappearing . . .

TOWN AND COUNTRY

By the 1980s, New Zealand rugby had taken on a distinctly urban flavour. All Black forwards were now the products of big city gymnasiums, not endless hours carrying a sheep under each arm across hill country farms. One of the great All Blacks of the 70s and 80s, Andy Haden, recalls running in work boots to the hill-tops of his parents' farm, but believes he represented the end of an era. Haden eventually became known as the All Blacks' unofficial shop steward — in charge of 'lurks and perks' — who maintained a dogged assault on the stuffy amateur traditions of the game, and later made a business out of representing the commercial interests of rugby players and other celebrities. But the transition from a game often associated with rugged farm boys to one of money and glamour was never more perfectly emblemised than in the rivalry between two men, Alex Wylie and John Hart; as coaches of the two great Ranfurly Shield teams of the 1980s, Canterbury and Auckland, and as competitors for the job of All Black coach (won by Wylie, with Hart joining him briefly during the ill-fated World Cup campaign in 1991; though Hart was successful in gaining the position at the end of 1995).

Wylie, known as Grizz, was the former All Black loose forward; gruff, media-shy and seemingly in the classic mould of rugby's long line of 'no comment' men. Hart, by contrast, was the garrulous Auckland halfback and now successful businessman; media-savvy, irreverent, full of the fashionable jargon of man-management filtering down from the corporate high-rises. In fact, the two men had their similarities. Both believed in and encouraged open, entertaining rugby, and both were great coaches in their own different ways. With Brian Lochore, they formed the selection panel for the unbeatable 1987 All Blacks.

One was the bluff Canterbury farmer and the other was the Auckland yuppie. John always hates being called a yuppie, but that was the image he gave, whether it was justified or not. They're two entirely different personalities. One was a hard man on the rugby field and a hard man off it, not

. . . irreverent, full of the fashionable jargon of man-management filtering down from the corporate high-rises.

117

given to eloquence or to many words at all. The other, John Hart, was a typical Auckland halfback, always smiling and talking. Just different people.

Ron Palenski

The Wylie-Hart battle was never symbolic of much more than the provincial bias of their respective supporters. However, Auckland rugby in the 1980s was beginning to display the characteristics of its hometown. The Auckland Union's executive director Lew Pryme had once been an entertainer and a show business promoter (as well as a rugby player), and Eden Park on match days began to look more like the Superbowl or the Winfield Cup grand final than a traditional Kiwi game of footy. There was bunting, there were cheerleaders, and there was music. Rugby, believe it or not, could be a carnival, and Pryme knew that to survive the game had to market itself as family entertainment, and not remain a clan gathering of pie-munchers and beer-guzzlers. Unlike the little towns of rural New Zealand, the big cities offered a greater variety of options for the discretionary dollar, and rugby had to compete like any other entertainment. As the biggest city, with its major port and airport, Auckland was also the country's meeting place with the rest of the world. A Pacific rim capital and a little city-state in its own right, it was home to diverse ethnic communities with their own interests and traditions. A brash merchant town from the very beginning, Auckland has never been overly sentimental about its own heritage.

I imagine in Otorohanga and Tuatapere and places like that it's much the same as it always was . . .

I imagine that rugby is still important to pockets of New Zealand culture, because parts of New Zealand haven't really changed all that much. So the further you get away from Auckland the more important it is. I imagine in Otorohanga and Tuatapere and places like that it's much the same as it always was, because it's a social quarter for small towns and country areas. But it's nowhere near as important as it was when I was young.

Warwick Roger

Even within Auckland, however, there were new reservoirs of talent and dedication to sustain big city rugby. One of the striking features of the game since the 1970s has been the influence of a fast-growing Pacific Island popu-lation. The photographs hanging around the walls of a club like Ponsonby show a gradual browning of teams dating from the late 1960s, when Samoan, Cook Island, Tongan, Niuean and other Island groups began migrating to New Zea-land in search of work. In Auckland and Wellington, these immigrant populations often experienced a dual exclusion from mainstream society. Having arrived with their extended family and church structures in place, they naturally resisted blunt assimilation, and meanwhile joined Maori and poor Pakeha at the bottom of the socio-economic scale, either working in poorly paid and insecure jobs, or being unemployed. The country's historical wariness of foreigners, given voice by the emphasis placed on allegedly illegal 'overstayers' by the Muldoon administration in the later 1970s, left Pacific Islanders with few points of normal contact with everyday New Zealand. In rugby, many found an entrée to the world of their Pakeha and Maori neighbours, and, in return, Pakeha and Maori came to understand a little of what these new New Zealanders had to offer.

> I suspect [I was] quite a role model, because when I first played for the All Blacks I was one of the few Polynesians at that stage who had made the All Blacks. After my career, we had this big surge of Polynesians making the All Blacks. People like Bernie Fraser and Inga [Tuigamala] and Joe Stanley. Currently many of them — Frank Bunce, Olo Brown, Walter Little, the Bachops, Michael Jones. And Jonah Lomu, the new sensation. It's something that obviously gives me a great deal of pride and satisfaction.
>
> *Bryan Williams*

. . . we had this big surge of Polynesians making the All Blacks.

One of the sensations of the 1991 World Cup was the emergence of the Western Samoan team — Manu Samoa, coached by Bryan Williams — as a force in world rugby. Samoa had, in fact produced the Solomon brothers, Frank and Dave (the latter born in Fiji), who were All Blacks in the 1930s. Frank was the last wing forward to play for New Zealand before the position was done away with. Dave turned to rugby league in 1939 and played for New Zealand on a British tour abandoned at the outbreak of the Second World War. Both, however, were educated in New Zealand, and they set a pattern for Samoan and Pacific Island players to follow. Brought from the islands by their parents, often for the educational opportunities, these children of the Pacific took to rugby like anyone growing up in a rugby land.

Among them was a boy who would become New Zealand's first Pacific Island member of parliament. Taito Phillip Field, MP for Otara, remembers playing around the small village Mulinuu, seat of the Western Samoan parliament, where his uncle worked as interpreter at the lands and title court. On the large front lawn of the radio station 2AP, the village kids would play with a coconut husk if there was no ball to be had, to the sound of church choirs recording at the station. Samoan rugby was nurtured in the schools run by Marist Brothers, and later through radio and television links with New Zealand. Eventually, a New Zealand-educated generation began returning to the island, taking

. . . the village kids would play with a coconut husk if there was no ball to be had . . .

with them their skills and enthusiasm for the game. The great All Black of the 1950s and 60s, Don Clarke, visited Samoa to coach after his playing career was over, and had a big impact in Apia particularly.

Field was raised by his grandmother after his parents migrated when he was six months old. They sent for him at age seven, and an uncle he barely knew accompanied him to Auckland on board the *Matua*, which with its sister ship the *Tofua* bore most migrants to New Zealand in the 60s and 70s. It was genuine culture shock. He arrived not speaking English, and not knowing his parents or his New Zealand-born, English-speaking siblings. From a village where they still used kerosene lamps to the big city lights; he remembers arriving at night and gazing in awe at so much electricity burning in one place — 'like arriving on a different planet'. In those days nearly every Samoan in Auckland would be there to meet the boat. A church service and a feast were followed by the train journey to Wellington, where he would grow up. He adapted well and learned the language, despite the lack of support for new immigrants. There weren't many Samoans at Cannons Creek Primary, so most of his first friends were Maori, and they played rugby. Field was in the primary school rep team with future All Black Murray Mexted, and remembers one of his early exposures to European culture, being billeted with a European family in Levin when his team won the championship. Later, at Tawa College, he again bumped into Mexted in the first fifteen, and again his team won the competition. He was selected for the Wellington secondary school rep team that played Fiji at Athletic Park in 1970.

Rugby provided 'the ability to perceive of working together to achieve a goal, culture and colour being irrelevant, just one team'. 'It was a common experience for Pacific Island kids. Because they were often good at the game, and physically matured faster than Europeans, they were judged on another level, not for their language difficulties or their differences. They were popular for their natural ability — for who they were. Many years later, when Field won the seat of Otara in 1993, the victory celebration was held at the home of Peter Fatialofa, captain of Manu Samoa. For many Pacific Islanders, says Field, doing well at rugby was their first experience of doing well at all in New Zealand. At the same time, New Zealanders were happy to hold aloft the new Pacific Island stars of rugby as their own, even if this did not always reflect a more general tolerance of the world from which such players sprang.

. . . doing well at rugby was their first experience of doing well at all in New Zealand.

Yes, we all took pride in what Jonah Lomu and players like him achieved at world level, but then we share the prejudice toward Pacific Island communities and areas like Otara and Mangere where people rang Telecom to complain about the fact that their real estate was going to be affected by having the same prefix telephone numbers as Otara. Well, it's these rugby stars who come from places like Otara and Mangere, and we are just as good as anybody else in New Zealand. So the way I look at it is that rugby has and will continue to play a role in breaking down those barriers.

Phillip Field

IMAGES OF SUCCESS

The growing disparity between rich and poor was obscured in the early stages of deregulation by the sheer scale of the change. Between 1984 and the sharemarket crash of October 1987, Auckland's skyline reflected the fact that the national economy had come to be dominated by the finance sector. Investment, lending and speculation were high, and the central city was remade in the mirrored image of fast, new money. As foreign capital flowed in, and the glass towers shot up, a fantasy developed that New Zealand was about to become a Switzerland of the South Pacific, a tiny financial powerhouse at the bottom of the world, producing financial services, not beef, butter and wool. Wishful thinking, of course, but symptomatic of a collective craving for success. When *KZ7*, the yacht of Auckland merchant banker Michael Fay (later Sir Michael), lost the challengers' series of the America's Cup in Fremantle, Australia, New Zealanders celebrated the crew's return with massive ticker-tape parades as if they had actually won.

Win or lose, the campaign did exhibit a self-confident willingness to mix it with all-comers, a kind of plucky-little-country syndrome that nurtured a belief in New Zealand's ability to compete on an equal footing (a 'level playing field' in the monetarist jargon of the time) with the world. In finance and in yachting the belief was, at best, optimistic (although another campaign in 1995 would finally lift the America's Cup for New Zealand). But in rugby, the traditional source of public self-esteem, the belief was warranted. After the nadir of the Springbok tour in 1981, followed by the ill-advised Cavaliers tour in 1986, New Zealand rugby had been forced to take stock. When the International Rugby Board permitted the Australian and New Zealand unions to devise and stage a world cup tournament for 1987, the game found its springboard into the modern era. Hastily organised, but largely successful, the inaugural Rugby World Cup was a triumph for an All Black team loaded with young talent of the likes of Michael Jones, John Kirwan, Wayne Shelford, Grant Fox, Sean Fitzpatrick and its photogenic young captain, David Kirk. Like Dave Gallaher, captain of the 1905

. . . a self-confident willingness to mix it with all-comers . . .

121

All Black 'Originals', Kirk embodied his era; a Rhodes scholar, a doctor, an aspiring businessman and a would-be politician, he instinctively understood the role of an All Black captain in a media-saturated world. Not just every mother's ideal son, but her ideal son-in-law too.

In the latter half of the 1980s, image became a lot more than just a public face. It was the commodity sought after by wealthy sponsors, and the vehicle for marketing their products to an audience of consumers (as opposed to citizens). Michael Fay's adventure had already shown the power of sponsorship to link ideas through association. The relative success of *KZ7* in the expensive, hi-tech, male-oriented world of yachting was sold as a metaphor for the achievement-oriented business culture that supported it. The hype became so frenzied at one stage, that the term 'blue water jingoism' was coined to describe it. In 1987, brewing giant Lion Nathan bought the right to associate its premium Steinlager brand with the internationally recognised All Black brand. It was the beginning of a sponsorship deal that would eventually see the red Steinlager label appear on the right breast of the All Black jersey, opposite the hallowed silver fern.

> We were looking for something that reflected Steinlager, or as we perceived Steinlager to be. So it was really a case of looking for a brand or a product, a sponsorship opportunity, and obviously the All Blacks became available. And there was, I'd have to say, heartache on the Rugby Union side as to whether one should ever allow sponsorship of New Zealand's premier team . . . I guess it was the commercialisation of the last bastion of New Zealand, or one of them, as there was when putting the actual logo onto the uniform — what are we doing here? What are we doing to this priceless thing? In actual fact, there wasn't a murmur when it actually happened.
>
> *advertising executive Robert Coulter*

> Huge lobbying went on for weeks beforehand to allow this to happen; the jersey's sacrosanct and all that sort of stuff. Colin Meads — we spoke to him about it — stood up at the annual general meeting [of the Rugby Union] with hundreds of these people from various unions, and said that he endorsed it . . . it was the way of the world, that it was commercial, and that it was going that way, and there wasn't a vote against it!
>
> *sports marketing manager Liz Dawson*

Commercial sponsorship was new to the Union and it was new to the players. In the build-up to the World Cup in 1987, Steinlager commissioned a television advertisement to launch their new association with the All Blacks. It was a sophisticated treatment of the physical qualities of the team, shot in a studio and

36.
The Kiwi festival. An Auckland supporter goes wild at the National Provincial Championship final at Eden Park, 1995. Meanwhile, three young rhythmic gymnasts and the Auckland mascot provide a surreal touch to the proceedings.

37.
*Young Auckland
supporters show their
colours at the NPC
final — rugby's
contribution to the
tribal instincts of
youth?*

38.
*Preparing for the big game —
and preparing to be ejected from
the big game. Some things
never change.*

39.
*Old rugby players never die —
they just dress up in bizarre
costumes. The Golden Oldies
parade in the square and later
play at grounds around
Christchurch. The one below is
at Hagley Park, 1995.*

40.
Proof that rugby's tribal rituals are at the core of its appeal. Face-painting and revelry before the Ranfurly Shield game between Auckland and Canterbury, Christchurch, 1995.

41.
Barbarians at the gate: Aucklanders invade Christchurch's green and pleasant land with their mock log of wood, and an over-enthusiastic fan is assisted from the ground during the game.

42.
A faint spectator is in danger of being over-looked for an interesting passage of play during the Ranfurly Shield match.

43.
An enterprising young
Canterbury fan snaps a self-
portrait with All Black Zinzan
Brooke as he leaves the field,
having helped Auckland defeat
the home team and regain the
Shield.

Animal effigies, strange runic
symbols, wizards . . . what
would a stranger make of the
off-field action that is known by
the all-purpose label, 'shield
fever'?

highly stylised to convey the Homeric properties of the All Black myth. It was set to the song 'Stand By Me' to reinforce the bonds within the team, and the need for public support on their World Cup campaign. In the language of sales and marketing, the Steinlager and All Black products were being positioned in the market. In historical terms, it was the beginning of the overt positioning of the All Blacks as a commodity and the players themselves as professionals. Although, at the time, the significance may have been lost on the boys in black.

> The players were ambivalent about the whole sponsorship thing . . . It wasn't that they didn't want to do it, it was kind of that they didn't really care whether they did it or not, or if they did it in the manner that you wanted them to do it . . . initially they were like children and animals. What I mean by that is, very, very difficult. They just do what they want to do. I was always surprised by how child-like, not necessarily childish, but how child-like they were. They were always playing games, telling jokes and laughing and fooling around. So to get them to actually stand still or do this or that, was very difficult. Very difficult!
>
> *Robert Coulter*

The novel presentation of the national icons in the finished advertisement made them appear at once human and superhuman, as bigger than ordinary men, but true mates in the mortal sense. It moved sociologist Nick Perry to describe it 'as if Colin Meads were to script Mills and Boon, having just seen Coppola's *Apocalypse Now* and Fassbinder's *Querelle*. In other words, it is camp.' Most viewers might not have taken this meaning from the clip, but the advertising agency's brief to make the All Blacks appealing to women led, according to Perry, to an alternative interpretation; '. . . insofar as it helps to explain such images as the close-up of Sean Fitzpatrick's narcissistic gaze into the camera lens, or the cutting up of men's bodies (thighs, waist-to-knee shots) in ways that have been made familiar by the portrayal of women in advertising . . . The resulting images are charged with sexual ambiguity. More particularly, they problematise the position of the heterosexual male viewer. He is confronted with Fitzpatrick's come-hither look or Michael Jones's flashing thighs, shot in lyrical slow motion that is characteristic of the portrayal of both sport replays and love-making. Whatever the intention, this commercial is clearly available for a distinctively gay reading.'

> I think it was making the guys look really attractive to the opposite sex. I mean, there was no real intention of trying to make it really attractive to

. . . it was the beginning of the overt positioning of the All Blacks as a commodity . . .

The resulting images are charged with sexual ambiguity.

women because rugby was, and probably still is, a very masculine sort of game. It appeals to males — it's by males, for males. So one had to be careful not to step over that boundary of people saying, oh poofters, you know? I mean, not rugby players! They don't look like that. It needed to be portrayed in a manner which was going to be acceptable to the public. And it was.

Robert Coulter

SELLING THE DREAM

Soon after the glamorisation of the All Blacks, another rather radical step was taken within the New Zealand Rugby Football Union. A woman, Liz Dawson, was hired as marketing manager. Dawson had been a sports fan all her life, and grew up watching her father and brother play rugby (although she opted later for the individualism of skiing over team games). When she applied for the Rugby Union post, she was employed by a food manufacturer, in charge of marketing ice-cream.

So it was to do with a lot of research into consumers' desires and what they wanted and how we could have a food product that fulfilled those desires. And so you take that to the next step and say, how does that fit the sport. Well, in fact, it's exactly the same thing, because people are very passionate about sport. New Zealanders are unbelievably passionate about sport. They have some desire, they have a want, they have a need, and the sporting organisations have got to fill that need.

Liz Dawson

The need to market rugby became increasingly obvious . . .

The need to market rugby became increasingly obvious as the commercial culture of deregulation spread into every corner of society. A report by the Boston Consulting Group (finally adopted in 1995), recommending the game's organisational structure be overhauled, that rule changes be implemented to make the game more attractive and that it should move towards professionalism, showed just how much the business ethos had invaded the fusty halls of the Rugby Union.

The recommendations were picked up more readily in the provinces than at the national level. In Hawke's Bay, where a love of rugby and allegiance to the provincial team could have been taken for granted right up until the 1970s, the union instigated a sweeping restructuring that mirrored what was taking place in the wider economy. As an All Black in the 1980s, Wayne Smith had become aware of the financial and time pressure on top players and the need for them to be rewarded in some way. Employers, faced with their own pressures, were less willing to employ top players merely for the reflected prestige. Through his friend John Kirwan, who had already played his off-seasons in Italy, Smith took a job as player-coach with a small club near Treviso, and later with the Treviso club itself. Treviso was sponsored by the giant fashion company, Bennetton, which had extensive commercial deals in sport, including its own Formula One racing team. Staying within the amateur code laid down by the International Rugby Board, Italian clubs still managed to attract foreign expertise and pay for it in airfares, accommodation and employment.

In return for his services, Smith learned a lot about 'quality, entertainment and the right way to treat people'. In stark contrast to New Zealand, there were 'no raffles, no meat pack prizes'. 'Not better,' he says of the Italian way, 'just different.' Similarly, being minnows in the rugby pond, the Italians tended to take a more analytical approach to the game. Smith learned to cut and edit training videos, how to develop mental skills in players. In 1993 the Hawke's Bay Union approached him to investigate marketing possibilities after the union was relegated to the second division of the national championship.

Smith accepted the position of chief executive with Hawke's Bay and, on the basis of a detailed marketing report he had put together, created a new union structure based on a corporate model with accountability its main aim. The early forays into marketing the team had mixed results — Smith says hiring a string quartet to play at one game 'went down like a lead balloon'. But with sponsors demanding to see proper financial plans before investing, there was no possibility that the old ways could survive.

The same values have permeated down to the club level. Still in the Hawke's Bay, the Taradale Club has tried to broaden its appeal by 'developing a mini-Australian leagues club system', according to manager Ian Cooper. 'When I got here it was singlets and gumboots,' he says of the clubrooms. Now there is a dress code, a variety of entertainments and food, and even a crèche on Saturday nights run by the women of an affiliated netball club. Like most clubs, the bulk of the money comes across the bar, where the sponsor's products are served to patrons who will, everyone hopes, associate the beer they are drinking with the fun they are having and the rugby they love.

The combination of beer and rugby is, in fact, a subtle concoction of myths and associations. As beer baron Douglas Myers puts it, both Steinlager and the All Blacks are 'tested in the market. It's not good enough for them to be seen to be. It's got to be.'

. . . a subtle concoction of myths and associations.

125

Over the last ten years, when New Zealand has been through a process of political and economic change, and when many in the community were obviously very upset and confused about the change, we felt it was very important for us as a New Zealand company to be involved with things like the All Blacks and yachting, that would give New Zealanders hope and confidence that we were going to come out the other side of this political reformation that we'd been through. And to remind us all that there is no reason whatsoever why New Zealand shouldn't be considered to be capable of performing at a world-class level in a whole range of activities.

Lion Nathan chief executive officer Douglas Myers

Richard Seddon would have understood. Douglas Myers, scion of one of Auckland's prominent business families, was a player himself. He made the first fifteen in his last year at King's College, a replica of the very kind of English public school from which rugby came, and played against Otahuhu College in the 1950s when its team included future All Blacks Mac Herewini and Waka Nathan. Rugby was compulsory — 'those that didn't [play] were wimps, as was the wont in New Zealand' — and as much a part of an all-round education as algebra or grammar. Like many others, he looks back on the 'golden era' of rugby as a deadeningly conformist time, when the grey blocks of the welfare state were being cemented into place, stifling the expression of individuality and talent. As chairman of the Business Roundtable, the political lobby group composed of the heads of most major business corporations, he has argued for the removal of state intervention in many areas of the economy and society. Not surprisingly, rugby, in the shape of the Rugby Union, was one of the last institutions to bow to this pressure.

. . . he looks back on the 'golden era' of rugby as a deadeningly conformist time . . .

I always used to say that it was the meat works and the breweries that were the two most decrepit industries, only because we'd been there longer. And probably of all New Zealand institutions, certainly in the sporting world, I guess the Rugby Union has been by far the strongest and the oldest, and the one that has played most poignantly with New Zealand's heart strings.

Douglas Myers

BREAD AND CIRCUSES

We're now starting to see rugby emerging not as a sport of those in, say, the United Kingdom, who went to the better universities, or in New Zealand who were a sort of provincial pedigree stock, or an urban, smart physical élite, but as people who sell their absolute ability and prowess. Which means that rugby has become no different from the best computer programmer, except that no computer programmer is ever photographed in underpants.

David Lange

Until 1995, when full professionalism was finally introduced, rugby players were unable to sell their talents on the open market. As late as 1978, Auckland Rugby Union chairman Ron Don was claiming that, 'Once rugby becomes professional, it is not rugby.' It was a sentiment dating back to the very origins of the game, to Victorian and Edwardian notions of the innate virtue of games. It seems remarkable that in the late twentieth century, the expression of Victorian class conflict as evidenced in the struggle over amateurism and professionalism could still be debated on a moral level. 'By and large the line between amateur and professional is mainly a line between the unpaid members of a privileged class, and the paid members of an underprivileged class,' wrote the American sports philosopher Paul Weiss. If so, the conflict had evolved in New Zealand into one between the administrators of the game and the players, scrapping over an issue with no genuine relevance in a modern consumer society.

Not that amateurism was the only Victorian notion being challenged in the last decade of the twentieth century. Wider concepts of the greater good were under attack from Maori, who began to assert their belief in the validity of the Treaty of Waitangi with renewed vigour. Pakeha ideas about sovereignty and racial partnership were put to the test, often by direct action and civil disobedience. There were calls for separate judicial systems, education systems, health services, even a separate parliament. Rugby was by no means immune. The under-representation of Maori at the administrative level, and the dwindling number of tours and internationals played by Maori teams, inspired many to wonder if a separate union might better represent Maori interests.

Go back a number of years to when the East Coast was reasonably strong. The team was comprised of 99 per cent Maori, but the administration was virtually a hundred per cent non-Maori. Even if you look at the modern-day Rugby Union, the whole union is made up of non-Maori people, with one Maori advisory person, not even appointed by Maori people . . . In the last fourteen years Maori have played only one home international and have been given two tours to appease them. In the past, Maori were always part of every visiting team's itinerary. I guess this has disenchanted Maori people a lot, although they still love the game of rugby. And the evidence that I offer for that is the number of Maori people who have gladly taken up league.

Given also that the professional cloak has been thrown over rugby, Maori as individual players might succeed. But Maori in general terms, as playing people, may not.

Jim Perry

. . . the whole union is made up of non-Maori people, with one Maori advisory person . . .

127

Maybe it's more than mere historical coincidence that the first calls for rugby players to be compensated came from a Maori. At the turn of the century, soon after the northern unions in England had broken away to form rugby league, Tom Ellison argued that players should be compensated for lost wages. Since his time, a nod-and-a-wink culture had slowly evolved to get around the amateur restrictions. As Harold Perkin wrote in an essay entitled 'Teaching the Nations How To Play', 'In the white dominions, always more democratic than the mother country, class differences were less obsessive, and the amateur/professional divide was taken less seriously. They soon found ways in the interest of technical performance and of beating England, of selecting and funding their best cricket and rugby players from any level of society.' It became known as 'shamateurism' and led to the absurd situation whereby top players could earn money promoting the game, but not playing it. In the 1980s, Australian entrepreneur David Lord tried to form a travelling rugby circus called World Championship Rugby, and before that a group calling itself World Professional Rugby Football (involving Lew Pryme) had proposed something similar. Neither venture got off the ground, but as time wore on, rugby appeared increasingly anachronistic in a world that took pro-sports for granted. Boxing, soccer, American football and baseball, basketball, athletics, motor racing, rugby league and tennis all made millionaires of their most talented exponents. When the dam finally broke for rugby after the 1995 World Cup, it was television that stood at the centre of the new money-go-round.

. . . it was television that stood at the centre of the new money-go-round.

THE BIG PICTURE

Typically, it was the southern hemisphere rugby nations, Australia and New Zealand, that forced the professional point. Historically less hidebound by the amateur ethic, and consistently the dominant national teams anyway, they entered the professional era at an interesting time in the development of global media organisations. The early 1990s had seen an enormous realignment of the large communications corporations, with a frenzy of takeovers and mergers as once distinct industries began to 'converge' at a technological level. Computer and telecommunications innovations now made it possible, and strategically logical, for cable television companies, phone companies, film production companies, hardware and software manufacturers, and publishers to join forces in the relentless pursuit of ever bigger audiences. Foremost among the new breed of ambitious international media barons was Rupert Murdoch, Australian born but now a citizen of the United States. With an American television network, satellite and newspaper empires in Britain and Europe, a Hong Kong-based Asian satellite TV network and TV and publishing interests in Australasia, Murdoch's News Corporation had the potential to cover most of the inhabited parts of planet Earth with its programmes. The $824 million Murdoch eventually paid for the television rights to southern hemisphere rugby meant he had a product around which to sell advertising. In the same year, Murdoch had ripped control of Australian rugby league from its traditional masters, buying clubs and players to form a new 'superleague' that he could market on his own television networks.

It was reminiscent of the way another media giant, Australian Kerry Packer, moved into cricket in the 1970s, creating the one-day game and breaking the stranglehold of the English establishment. (It was also Kerry Packer who stood behind a rival deal to Murdoch's when the shift to professional rugby descended into a contract war for players, and it was Packer's Channel Nine that stood to suffer most from Murdoch's raid on rugby league transmission rights.) When Packer first put his cricket plans to the Victorian Cricket Association in 1976, he reportedly said to the assembled administrators, 'We're all harlots, how much do you want?' Maybe not surprisingly, he bought a fight, but he never pretended that it was over anything more than television rights. With doggedness and deep pockets, he eventually won, and cricket became a massive revenue source for Channel Nine. In the 1990s, tests and one-day internationals regularly pulled in half to two-thirds of available viewers.

Television programmers have long understood the desirability of sport. It is a form of drama that suits the small screen perfectly. Its outcomes are unpredictable, increasing its power to capture and hold an audience. It comes prepackaged in tight time formats, with space for advertising in and around each game. It is cheap to broadcast compared with drama or news. And most importantly, the people who follow sport keenly are exactly the 'demographic' that television companies want to sell to advertisers; they are male (but by no means exclusively), relatively well-educated, and with considerable disposable income.

. . . he had a product around which to sell advertising.

Sport has this wonderful advantage over drama. It has no script. You don't know what the outcome's going to be. No matter how many bad games you see of one-day cricket, no matter how many ends, third acts that don't happen, you still go back to the possibility that it could happen next time.
Greg McGee

129

> We talk about entertainment on TV, we talk about ratings, we don't talk about crowd numbers. The audience has changed. We're consumers, we're not just the faithful turning up to the game.
>
> *Lloyd Jones*

Rugby's transformation into a packaged television entertainment was accelerated in New Zealand by the deregulation of broadcasting in the late 1980s. The previously commercial but state-governed television channels became a 'state owned enterprise', whose statutory mission was to turn a profit and return a dividend to its shareholder, the government. The new commercial imperative brought with it a new programmer, poached from the competitive world of private radio in Auckland, John McCready. McCready had also worked for many years in the Australian music industry, and had become a convert to the highly televisual sport of Winfield Cup rugby league. New Zealand television, once the undisputed domain of rugby union, was now contested territory.

I wanted to bring that to rugby as well. I wanted to make rugby more accessible to a female and a family audience.

> I'm 55 years old. I was brought up in the great era of rugby when to be an All Black when you were a young boy was everything. So your whole life revolved around the local football club. But it's a very macho-man, male-dominated thing. What I saw in Sydney was the fact that families and women went along to rugby league and enjoyed it as a day's outing . . . And really, I wanted to bring that to rugby as well. I wanted to make rugby more accessible to a female and a family audience.
>
> *John McCready*

McCready began by placing a woman, Julie Christie, in charge of sport at Television New Zealand, putting a number of male noses out of joint in the process. Rugby was repackaged as an entertainment, and pointed towards a market niche on one channel, while the other, ostensibly more commercial, channel was given over to rugby league. Just as Lion Breweries targeted its rugby audience with an upmarket beer brand (Steinlager) and league with a downmarket brand (Lion Red), so too was television divided into market segments.

In 1989, McCready broadcast the final of the Winfield Cup live from Sydney, drawing a massive audience, running over time (not generally condoned in the strictly formatted world of programming), and establishing once and for all that rugby union could no longer assume, as if by divine right, that it was the only game in town. Like so much of what happened in the 1980s, it had its genesis in the reaction to the conformist society in which the children of the baby boom grew up.

44.
The beginnings of the big time for many boys. A grim winter's day in West Auckland, and the trials for the Champion Roller Mills team is underway. Later, in the Waitemata clubrooms, the squad listens to its first team talk. Photographs in this section by George Andrews.

45.
The national pastime. Aucklanders enjoy a beer at the International Rugby Hall of Fame while watching their team take the Ranfurly Shield off Canterbury. Meanwhile, the Ponsonby clubroom winds into a cheerful aftermatch drinking session after the day's matches.

46.
Spot the Canterbury supporters in Auckland as the Shield slips away. The International Rugby Hall of Fame resides in Rugby Plaza, downtown Auckland, formerly Finance Plaza, a glass and steel monument to the 1980s sharemarket boom. Maybe the national game seemed a safer bet in the 1990s, but by early 1996 the Hall was suffering from lower than expected patronage.

47.
Brett Kamutoa (centre, with plaited hair) listens as the Roller Mills squad is announced. Brett is in, but others aren't. The best of times, the worst of times. Yes, that's Bryan Williams at far left, whose own son also made the grade. Will it all lead to the scene below? Aucklanders celebrate the Shield's return north.

I always felt as a young man that rugby was the most important thing in our lives as young males. I didn't think that was too healthy personally. I was a sports person who liked rugby league, I liked gymnastics, I liked ice-skating. And I found it was an unhealthy peer pressure, as far as I was concerned, to conform. I saw that as part of the whole New Zealand psyche, that I really resented being imposed upon as an individual.

John McCready

The enlarged audience for rugby league that McCready helped create led eventually to the inclusion of Auckland in the Winfield Cup competition. New Zealand players were already prominent in the Australian clubs, more than a few of them defectors from rugby union, lured by the money they could never make in their first game of choice. The arrival of the Auckland Warriors in 1995 gave further notice that the attention and allegiance of floating sports fans were up for grabs. Warriors chief executive Ian Robson, who learned his trade managing Australian Rules clubs, brashly predicted that there would one day 'be a generation of Kiwi kids that didn't know who came first — the Warriors or the All Blacks'. In another sign of things to come, Warriors games were telecast live only on the pay-TV Sky Network.

. . . the attention and allegiance of floating sports fans were up for grabs.

The club lured Liz Dawson away from rugby to manage its marketing. The Warriors home games were sellouts. In its first year, the club signed up five former All Blacks, including one after rugby itself had gone professional. Old rugby fans commented on the atmosphere at Ericsson Stadium compared to the lukewarm crowds at many interprovincial rugby matches. The sport is tailor-made for television, being an almost continuous (if sometimes monotonous) flow of action, free from the scrum and lineout delays of union. The Warriors themselves became celebrities, not just in Auckland but right around the country. They were immediately media-friendly. And most interestingly, they appealed to women.

What brings a modern woman to watch rugby league? It's about heroes, and it's about sex. It's about attractiveness and the fine athlete. And there's a bit of protectiveness about it, you know, being able to perform miracles on the field — strength and vitality and not in the macho sort of way, but in a very masculine way that's attractive to females. Whereas with rugby, it's still so much a male sport and a male-supported sport because the players don't portray the same things as rugby league players do.

Liz Dawson

But there is no simple equation here. At the same time as rugby has drifted from the centre of national life, it has been taken up by groups at what were once the peripheries of its influence. Women no longer play it as a novelty, but compete as proper teams within established clubs for their own trophies. As Tracy Lemon of the Ponsonby Club in Auckland explains, the very plenitude of options that pulls others away from rugby, has created the climate that allows women to choose rugby as their preferred game. Schools offering rugby to girls, the phenomenal success of touch rugby, and the general fallout of mainstream feminism have all helped break down the old stereotype that the bottom of a ruck was no place for a lady. From a distance, the changing-room and the playing field look remarkably similar, regardless of the sex of those wearing the shorts. In the process, clubs have been further democratised, and also increased their player and funding base. It's a wonderful irony that in the 1990s it's often the children on the sideline cheering their mothers on, not the reverse.

> A lot of the time the girls have to bring their kids along to watch, and they just have to be there, because their husbands are either at their own training or at work. I mean, the kids love it. They run around, they have a good time. It's fine, it's not a problem.
>
> *Tracy 'Chuckey' Lemon*

In the end, it was all about consumer choice . . .

In the end, it was all about consumer choice, one of the fundamental tenets of the free market creed. In the protected and media-insulated New Zealand of the 1950s, rugby's hegemony was virtually guaranteed. In the 1990s it was inevitably undermined by the sheer variety of information available via the new media. Society's fragmentation into niche markets actively conspired against rugby's once common appeal. Of course, the free market comes with one obvious caveat — one's choice is limited by one's ability to pay for it. A free market consumer society places its emphasis on individual choice far more than communal aspiration. Rugby may yet maintain its grip, especially through the continued commitment of traditional schools to the game. But in a world that celebrates and rewards individual achievement, that has spurned the underlying values of a socialist model of collective well-being, it will increasingly become just another option in the lifestyle supermarket — albeit a popular one.

> My perception is that a middle-class child is less likely to pull on a team jersey in any sport, than to go for some sort of designer sports or recreational wear — wind-surfing, skiing, surfing, that kind of thing . . . I've got two boys who are 12 and 10, and sometimes I feel like I'm an immigrant from a country that's no longer visible. Because they have no interest in rugby and wonder why I can get so excited about watching this game, because they

don't see rugby in their upbringing. They live on a hill. What are their sports? They go swimming, they like rock climbing. There's not this passion for a game that was in my life and in the lives of my contemporaries.

Lloyd Jones

And I found it was an unhealthy peer pressure, as far as I was concerned, to conform.

THE GAME OF OUR LIVES

Does Brett Kamutoa see any real difference between league and rugby players? 'No, not really.' Brett has grown up in a world where talented football players switch codes for money, not love. A world where the Warriors look just as exciting on the TV screen as do the All Blacks. By the time he finishes high school, rugby will have been professional for six or seven years. As a Champion Roller Mills player he has already moved out ahead of the pack, and might one day even earn a living from spinning the ball from the back of the scrum. Right now, though, he still thinks you need a proper career, not just a bunch of rugby dreams.

At the Eden prizegiving, Ray Quickfall takes time to reflect on his 32 years' association with the club. In that time he has served in every administrative position, and even now he mucks in to wipe the tables and empty the ashtrays. The club, he reckons, is all about keeping the youngsters off the street — a role it can fulfil all year round, now that touch rugby takes over in the summer. On the other hand, the kids 'are more difficult to look after now. There's so much for them to do, apart from rugby. When I first started there was rugby and that was about it.'

Only a few weeks after the prizegiving, Ray Quickfall died. In tribute to the man who had done so much for the club, Eden supporters and players turned out on the day of his funeral to say goodbye. The wake — dubbed the 'aftermatch' — was held back at the same clubrooms, where so many young boys had received their first glimpse of the rewards and companionship that rugby can offer. The cycle of life and death and rugby goes on.

All over New Zealand there are people like Ray Quickfall — it's a cliché only because it's true, but they are the unsung heroes of rugby. As the commercial imperative bites deeper into the game and the society that sustains it, it remains to be seen whether a new generation will come to replace them — whether the team can survive in the age of the individual. New Zealand rugby was only ever great because of a willing volunteer spirit, a selfless dedication to the mundane tasks of running a club; the marking of fields, the washing of jerseys, the building of clubrooms and the coaching of kids. When everything has its price, what is

New Zealand rugby was only ever great because of a willing volunteer spirit, a selfless dedication to the mundane . . .

133

the price of that? As one of the long-serving members of a rural rugby club put it, 'Young guys these days only want to know what the club can do for them, not what they can do for the club.'

There are few rational arguments to be made against the advent of professionalism. Even those who believe passionately in the amateur ethic, and who despair now that rugby has become just like every other commercialised code, tend to reach for words that aren't there when pressed to justify their position. Who in all fairness would deny a man whose only great talent is an ability to kick or run with a ball, the chance to earn a living from that if the chance is there? And who would seriously defend the cosy lifestyles of an administrative élite, who once ate better food than players at official functions, and who drew their stipends from the money generated by the efforts of amateurs on the field? Indeed, as the millennium nears, who in New Zealand would look at the trappings of English tradition and think they were anything more than quaint?

. . . the game's capacity to excite and galvanise was as potent as ever.

On the face of it, the tribal rituals of rugby are indestructible. When Canterbury defended the Ranfurly Shield against Auckland in 1995, and lost, the game's capacity to excite and galvanise was as potent as ever. Why else do grown men stage mock fights in bars over drip-cloths in another province's colours? Or go to the trouble of dressing a mannequin in the team stripe and stringing it from a gibbet? The game is still, in the immortal words from Greg McGee's *Foreskin's Lament*, 'the heart and the bowels of this country'.

What might be at risk, however, is whatever it is about rugby that people take for granted. Maybe it doesn't have a name, or a function, or a price. Maybe it's just what kept people coming down to the ground on a Saturday before money was an object. The thing that kept people playing long after it was obvious that the big-time would never come. The reason people stayed with a club, even when the season's last game was always a play-off for last. The pleasures of winning when there's nothing to win, or losing when there's nothing left to lose. And maybe it is simply inevitable that it be lost, whatever it is. All things change. Rugby is no exception.

Bibliography

Barry, Paul, *The Rise and Rise of Kerry Packer*, Bantam/ABC, Sydney, 1993

Blainey, Geoffrey, *A Game of Our Own: The Origins of Australian Football*, Information Australia, Melbourne, 1990

Buchanan, Timothy N W, 'Missionaries of Empire: The 1905 All Black Tour', essay, University of Canterbury department of history, 1981

Carmen, Arthur H, *Maori Rugby*, Sporting Publications, Wellington, 1980

Chester, R H, McMillan N A C & Palenski R A, *The Encyclopaedia of New Zealand Rugby*, Moa, Auckland, 1981

Coney, Sandra, 'Oh, My Papa!', in *Between the Posts: A New Zealand Rugby Anthology*, Hodder and Stoughton, Auckland, 1989

Coney, Sandra, *Standing in the Sunshine*, Penguin, Auckland, 1993

Crawford, Scott A G M, 'Muscles and Character Are There the First Object of Necessity: an overview of sport and recreation in a colonial setting', in the *British Journal of Sports History*, Vol. 2, London, 1985

Dix, John, *Stranded in Paradise*, Paradise Publications, Auckland, 1988

Downes, Peter, and Harcourt, Peter, *Voices in the Air*, Methuen, Wellington, 1976

Fougere, Geoff, 'Sport, Culture and Identity: the Case of Rugby Football', in *Culture and Identity in New Zealand*, Government Print, 1989

Graham, Jeanine, 'Settler Society', in *The Oxford History of New Zealand*, 2nd edn, Oxford University Press, Auckland, 1992

Hall, Fiona, J, 'The Greater Game: Sport and Society in Christchurch During the First World War', thesis, University of Canterbury, 1989

King, Michael, *New Zealanders At War*, Heinemann Reed, Auckland, 1981

Macrory, Jenny, *Running With the Ball: The Birth of Rugby Football*, Collins Willow, London, 1991

McCarthy, Winston, *Haka! The All Blacks Story*, Pelham, London, 1968

McGee, Greg, *Foreskin's Lament* (Foreword by Michael Neil), Victoria University Press, Wellington, 1981

McLauchlan, Gordon, *The Passionless People*, Cassell, Auckland, 1976

Mulgan, John, *Report on Experience*, Oxford University Press, Auckland, 1984

Nepia, George, & McLean, Terry, *I, George Nepia*, Reed, Wellington, 1963

Newnham, Tom, *A Cry of Treason; New Zealand and the Montreal Olympics*, Dunmore, Palmerston North, 1978

Olssen, Erik, 'Towards a New Society', in *The Oxford History of New Zealand* 2nd edn, Oxford University Press, Auckland, 1992

Palenski, Ron, *Our National Game*, Moa, Auckland, 1992

Perkin, Harold, 'Teaching the Nations How to Play: Sport and Society in the British Empire and Commonwealth', in the *International Journal of the History of Sport*, Vol. 6, London, 1989

Perry, Nick, *The Dominion of Signs*, Auckland University Press, Auckland, 1994

Phillips, J O C, 'Rugby, War and the Mythology of the New Zealand Male', in *New Zealand Journal of History*, Vol. 18 (2), 1984

Richardson, Len, 'Rugby, Race, and Empire: The 1905 All Black Tour', in *Historical News*, No. 47, University of Canterbury, 1983

Ryan, G J, 'The Originals: The 1888-89 New Zealand Native Football Team in Britain, Australia and New Zealand', thesis, University of Canterbury, 1992

Sinclair, Keith, *Walter Nash*, Auckland University Press/Oxford University Press, Auckland, 1976

Sparks, Allister, *The Mind of South Africa: The Story of the Rise and Fall of Apartheid*, Heinemann, London, 1990

Thompson, Richard, *Retreat from Apartheid: New Zealand's Sporting contacts with South Africa*, Oxford University Press, Wellington, 1975

Walker, Ranginui J, 'Maori People Since 1950', in *The Oxford History of New Zealand*, 2nd edn, Oxford University Press, Auckland, 1992

Wenner, Lawrence A., *Media, Sports and Society*, Sage, California, 1989

Wilson, Neil, *The Sports Business*, Judy Piatkus, London, 1988

Wright-St Clair, Rex E, *Thoroughly a Man of the World — A Biography of Sir David Monro*, Whitcombe & Tombs, Christchurch, 1971

Index